BFI BRITISH SCREEN STORIES

SERIES EDITORS: Mark Duguid and Patrick Russell, BFI

The British Screen Stories series provides a unique guide to key genres within the history of British film and television. Rooted in, and richly illustrated with, material from the BFI's unique archive, the books lead readers through this fascinating terrain, expanding our understanding of familiar genres and enabling the discovery of those less well-known.

Each book focuses on a key aspect of British film and television, written in an authoritative yet accessible style. Extensive use of stills and other archive materials that tell new stories about our film heritage complement the text. A distinctive aspect is the 'Close-up' features interspersing each book. These features illustrate a particular topic through a case study, technique or aesthetic development using a concise, direct and strong visual narrative approach.

TITLES IN THE SERIES

The Story of British Animation by **Jez Stewart**
The Story of Victorian Film by **Bryony Dixon**
The Story of British Propaganda Film by **Scott Anthony**
The Story of British Video Activism by **Ed Webb-Ingall**

BRITISH SCREEN STORIES

THE STORY OF BRITISH VIDEO ACTIVISM

Ed Webb-Ingall

THE BRITISH FILM INSTITUTE
Bloomsbury Publishing Plc, 50 Bedford Square, London, WC1B 3DP, UK
Bloomsbury Publishing Inc, 1359 Broadway, New York, NY 10018, USA
Bloomsbury Publishing Ireland, 29 Earlsfort Terrace, Dublin 2, D02 AY28, Ireland
BLOOMSBURY is a trademark of Bloomsbury Publishing Plc

First published in Great Britain 2026 by Bloomsbury
on behalf of the
British Film Institute
21 Stephen Street, London W1T 1LN
www.bfi.org.uk

The BFI is the lead organisation for film in the UK and the distributor of Lottery funds for film. Our mission is to ensure that film is central to our cultural life, in particular by supporting and nurturing the next generation of filmmakers and audiences. We serve a public role which covers the cultural, creative and economic aspects of film in the UK.

Copyright © Ed Webb-Ingall, 2026

Ed Webb-Ingall has asserted his right under the Copyright, Designs and Patents Act, 1988,
to be identified as author of this work.

For legal purposes the Acknowledgements on p. 7 constitute an extension of this copyright page.

Cover design by Louise Dugdale
Cover image: Cover photograph taken during filming of
Liberation Films' *Starting to Happen* (1974), courtesy of Ron Orders.

All rights reserved. No part of this publication may be: i) reproduced or transmitted in any form, electronic or mechanical, including photocopying, recording or by means of any information storage or retrieval system without prior permission in writing from the publishers; or ii) used or reproduced in any way for the training, development or operation of artificial intelligence (AI) technologies, including generative AI technologies. The rights holders expressly reserve this publication from the text and data mining exception as per Article 4(3) of the Digital Single Market Directive (EU) 2019/790.

Bloomsbury Publishing Plc does not have any control over, or responsibility for, any third-party websites referred to or in this book. All internet addresses given in this book were correct at the time of going to press. The author and publisher regret any inconvenience caused if addresses have changed or sites have ceased to exist, but can accept no responsibility for any such changes.

A catalogue record for this book is available from the British Library.

ISBN: HB: 978–1–8390–2224–1
PB: 978–1–8390–2223–4
ePDF: 978–1–8390–2222–7
eBook: 978–1–8390–2221–0

Series: British Screen Stories

Designed, typeset and packaged by Tom Cabot/ketchup
Printed and bound in India

For product safety related questions contact productsafety@bloomsbury.com.

To find out more about our authors and books visit www.bloomsbury.com
and sign up for our newsletters.

CONTENTS

    Acknowledgements 7
    British Screen Stories: Editors' Introduction 9

    Introduction 11

1. Video Happenings 20
    Close-up: The Sony Portapak 32

2. See Yourself on TV! 34
    Close-up: Community Arts and the Basement Project 54
    Montage: Have a Go and Pass it on 56

3. Housing for All 58
    Close-up: From Newsreel to *Reel News* 80

4. Starting to Happen 82
    Close-up: Inter-Action and the Media Van 100

5. The People's Account 102
    Close-up: The Miners' Campaign Tapes 130
    Montage: Distribution Catalogues 132

6. Getting the Word Out 134
    Close-up: AIDS Activist Video 158

Epilogue: Video Activism 2.0 160

Further Reading 164
Playlist 166
Notes 168
Index 179
Illustration Credits 184

ACKNOWLEDGEMENTS

I would like to thank Mark Duguid and Patrick Russell at the BFI for their commitment to a largely unexplored aspect of UK film history, and Bloomsbury's Rebecca Barden, Anna Coatman and Barbara Cohen Bastos and designer Tom Cabot for their support. This book began as a PhD project in 2014, when my supervisors were Mandy Merck, who took a chance on my proposal and who worked tirelessly to develop it into a first draft, and Tony Dowmunt, who shared his knowledge and experience as a community videomaker and provided support and enthusiasm throughout my PhD project and beyond.

Throughout this project I have been fortunate enough to call upon the memories and reflections of Thomas Waugh, Carry Gorney, Ron Orders, Caroline Goldie, Tony Wickert, Peter Bloch, Keith Griffiths, Andy Porter, Heinz Nigg, John 'Hoppy' Hopkins, Mark Harriott, Paul O'Connor, Phillip Timmins, Jes Benstock, David Curtis, Femi Otitoju, Isaac Julien, Sue Hall and Su Braden, who were kind of enough to answer all of my questions and encourage me to ask more. It was thanks to the personal archives of many of these activists that I was able to piece together this history and help to establish the London Community Video Archive.

I am grateful for the financial support of a full scholarship from TECHNE and the administrative support from the staff in the Department of Media Arts at Royal Holloway, University of London, which made it possible for me to undertake my doctoral project. I received further support from the Paul Mellon Postdoctoral Fellowship in 2019, which allowed me to carry out research into AIDS Activist Video in the UK. Thanks to Nathaniel Jezzi and Jacob Blandy who patiently read through early drafts and provided invaluable feedback. I am also thankful to Ben Cook at LUX, Lucy Reynolds at MIRAJ and Laura Mulvey and Sue Clayton, who invited me to develop my thoughts into written and published works, as well as to Massimiliano Mollona, Nina Wakeford, Michael Birchall, Gail Pickering, Anna Colin, Louise Shelly and Margaret Salmon, who invited me to share my research and try out my ideas early on.

Throughout this project I have sought out and highlighted many forms of activism and am thankful to my mum, Caryle Webb-Ingall, who taught me the power of speaking out and challenging injustice. I have been inspired and encouraged by my personal involvement with grassroots activism as part of Housing Action and Southwark and Lambeth and Switchboard LGBTQIA+ Support Line. It was my friends and peers who always showed interest in my research and supported me to finish this project: Laura Guy, Naomi Pearce, Onyeka Igwe, Astrid Goldsmith, Markland Starkie, Holly Wood, Charlotte Procter, Claire Louise Staunton, Jamie Crewe, Mason Leaver Yap, Holly White, Rehana Zaman, Olivia Plender, Elsa Richardson, Irene Revell, Conal McStravick and, finally, Robbie Ellen, who has known me for the duration of this project and whose support will last a lifetime

BRITISH SCREEN STORIES: EDITORS' INTRODUCTION

Some 130 years since the first films flickered onto the screen, moving images dominate our lives. Our workplaces, schools and homes – even the journeys between them – are saturated with film.

So how did we get here? What's the story? Or rather, the stories – because film contains multitudes. Moving images preceded the cinema, found a new home on television, and began to fill the online space as soon as capacities allowed. Today, most of us carry a cinema in our pocket. And film has always taken countless forms, performed many different functions and (intentionally or not) elicited numerous effects. From the start, films have entertained, informed and educated, but also provoked, disturbed, challenged, experimented, aroused, recorded, reported, promoted, sold, persuaded and deceived.

This dizzying variety is an enduring feature of film, linking its present to its past and its future. Digital technology has transformed the ways moving images are produced, distributed and consumed, and the volume of screen 'content' has skyrocketed. But while almost none has ever seen a strip of celluloid, today's 'films' – be they features or television programmes, adverts or pop videos, gallery installations or TikToks – share a common ancestor in the first moving images to dazzle 1890s audiences.

As studios and broadcasters mine their back catalogues and public archives – who have been conscientiously preserving film heritage for many decades – open up their vaults with mass digitisation initiatives, so much that was previously largely hidden from public view is now available on a device near you. Britain has been in the vanguard of this digitisation revolution.

For example, the BFI National Archive now holds over 300,000 digitised items (on top of many more acquired in digital form). The borders between past and present are collapsing, as are the boundaries between the mainstream and what were once assumed to be niche tastes. Silent newsreels and CGI blockbusters, 19th-century street scenes and 21st-century vlogs: all these and countless more now sit side-by-side on video streaming platforms.

This sudden superabundance demands a redrawing of the boundaries of what film in Britain is, while laying bare just how much remains unmapped. This series strives to explore this territory, telling fresh stories, retelling and revitalising familiar ones in the light of new discoveries and shining a light on overlooked or undervalued sectors, traditions and genres of British filmmaking.

The fourth book in this series, Ed Webb-Ingall's *The Story of Video Activism*, shows how the emergence of a new moving image technology – the first to rival celluloid – had a radical and democratising effect on media and politics. Videotape, with its relatively portable and affordable cameras and equipment and its easier playback and distribution, offered access to voices, viewpoints and demographics under-represented in established moving image forms and industries.

This book tells the story of video activism, an early innovation of the videotape era, from its 1960s countercultural origins through the political struggles of the following decades. Webb-Ingall explores how the technical properties of tapes and equipment shaped activist filmmaking in a variety of different settings. As he shows, the pioneer video activists, using physical tape as their medium, were the analogue ancestors of today's digital campaigners, who make extensive use of tapeless moving image technology.

Ed Webb-Ingall is a filmmaker, academic and curator who, not least as a founder of the London Community Video Archive, has been at the forefront of preserving often vulnerable material from the risk of damage or loss, while championing and making available the work of the pioneering generations of video activists. Challenging decades of neglect in mainstream accounts of non-fiction filmmaking in Britain, his book mounts its own campaign for the recognition not only of video activism's impact as a political tool, but of the true value of its practitioners' contribution to screen history.

Mark Duguid & Patrick Russell

INTRODUCTION

One of the most exciting new movements for anyone concerned with social change or visual media is the application of video.

'Video in Community Development',
the Centre for Advanced Television Studies, 1972

In 1965, Sony, one of the earliest producers of domestic and portable video cameras, published a playful magazine advert listing the potential uses the company envisaged for its latest product, the TCV-2010 Videorecorder. The technology meant that, for the first time (and in contrast to film), moving image, with synchronised sound, could be recorded then, at the push of a button, instantly played back. The focus of Sony's advert was on recording videos for repeated playback: improving a golf swing, studying (or ogling) a favourite film or TV star, fast-forwarding through advert breaks, perfecting wedding speeches, delivering workplace presentations, capturing precious family milestones and collecting together clip compilations for posterity. It's a disappointingly pedestrian list, which barely hints at the radical transformations that domestic video would unleash.

By the end of the 1960s, video had become the industry standard in television production, allowing for more efficient and streamlined processes for recording and transmitting programmes. The introduction of video into the domestic sphere in the 1970s would profoundly change how people viewed, experienced, collected and created moving images. Beyond the more homely uses Sony had its sights set on, video invited experimentation in new forms of moving image production and distribution.

study how to strike Mickey Mantle out	measure Miss Universe's ankles	record the nostril dilation of a passionate actress	film your son receiving graduation honors*
perfect your golf by watching the Golden Bear in action	practice a foreign language lesson 100,000 times (if you're slow)	mock Bernstein conducting an orchestra	see who sweats the most at the U.N.
catch the slips of famous personalities	become a film editor and producer*	recall how Bobby Kennedy reacted under pressure	collect the scenic wonders of many nations
study how-to-do-it techniques for your home and garden	record the cars that stalled at Indianapolis	watch movie without a single break	catch the tension of Louis Armstrong's cheeks while he's playing
copy the pattern of Glen Gould's socks	see how many opera singers have bridges	polish up your delivery of an important speech*	put together your own sequences of the best in T.V.
compare the tear channels of your favorite actresses	build a complete, private theater repertory	get rid of all commercials from your favorite shows	

A picture, someone said, is worth a thousand words. So we say no more. Just get to see SONY's exciting Videocorder which records and plays back video and audio signals for American black-and-white TV standards. A single tape runs a full hour. Portable, transistorized and smartly styled, the SONY Videocorder will add more life to your life. *And SONY's Video Camera is the ideal accessory.

SONY

Selling the Sony TCV-2010 Videocorder (print advertisement, 1965).

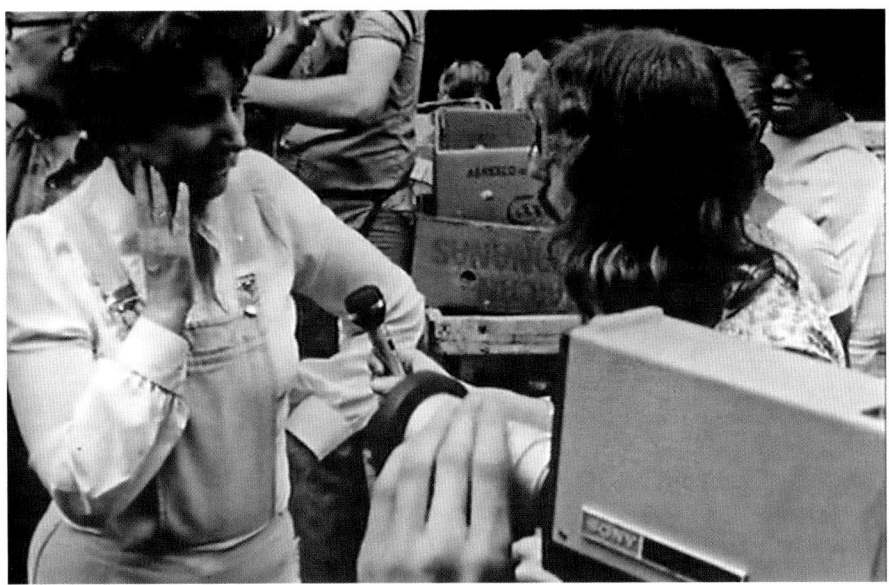

Starting to Happen (Liberation Films, 1973).

It's no surprise, then, that Sony's advert makes no mention of documenting or facilitating oppositional activist video projects. And yet video activists would be among the earliest adopters of the new technology. Around the same time, these same portable video cameras were being deployed to record the lives of marginalised and underrepresented groups, activating social and political change on squatted streets, rundown housing estates and adventure playgrounds built on reclaimed land.

In 1972, a collective of radical London-based media activists established the Centre for Advanced Television Studies and published 'Video in Community Development'. This practical handbook on the use of video by grassroots groups was the first document published in the UK to describe what would come to be known as 'activist video'. The back-cover blurb of this academic-looking pamphlet explains that 'the portable video-tape recorder has at last made television a fast and cheap medium which can be used at street level'.[1]

The first activist videos were black-and-white, with fuzzy, low-contrast images, largely featuring scruffy-looking 'drop-outs', elderly council tenants and working-class kids. The picture was broken up by flickering horizontal lines and, when the camera was moved too fast in bright light, a ghostly imprint of the previous image lingered. To capture sound, producers could choose either a built-in microphone, which allowed for a running commentary describing the action unfolding on screen, or a handheld microphone, which invited the pose – but not the pomp – of a TV news reporter, and enabled questions to be asked in front of the camera. The soundtrack was accompanied by a background hum and the intermittent clicks and whirs of the reels on the video recorder unit as the tape was stopped and started.

Video arrived during a resurgence of left-wing political activity and social change. For many young people coming of age in the UK in the late-1960s the era was a time of instability: industrial unrest, student occupations and marches against nuclear weapons, as well struggles for equality in race, gender and sexuality. In the US, the same period was marked by a series of high-profile political assassinations, race riots and protests against the ongoing Vietnam War (which also made their way to the UK). The result was a growing mistrust of and opposition to the political and social order. By the

Framed Youth: Revenge of the Teenage Perverts (Lesbian and Gay Youth Video Project, 1983).

The Disabling Council (Albany Video, 1987).

early 1970s, what was left of the 'peace and love' of the 1960s was swiftly being replaced by something angrier and more combative. This new movement was largely rooted outside of party politics, with a focus on single-issue and localised concerns and the day-to-day activities of self-organised groups. Video was a new and as yet unexplored medium that offered a means for these groups to question and challenge established, top-down modes of mass communication that, more often than not, sought to misrepresent and exclude them.

For those whose voices were routinely ignored or silenced by mainstream media, video came to be seen in almost utopian terms, as a powerful tool to document and share their experiences on their own terms. Women's groups, teenagers, gay liberationists, tenants' associations, those on low or no income and Black and global majority people all now had the means to represent themselves. They were able to conceive formal approaches that reflected their identification with the subject located in front of the camera and to produce videos that could intervene in the lived experience of those involved. The audience could become a collaborator in media activism, where video's capacity to represent experiences was often a prelude to community organising – as well as vice versa.

Activist videos have never been a replacement for social and political action. What the story of video activism makes clear, however, is how much the production, distribution and exhibition of activist video projects can contribute to social and political change. Those involved in making activist videos understand the significance of the interpersonal aspects of their work, placing importance on having direct connections with the groups and experiences they seek to represent and fight for and alongside.

Video activism was initially referred to as 'community video', and had its roots in the wider community arts movement, its experimental aesthetic tendencies emerging alongside the birth of video art. 'Activist video' is a slippery term, characterised by activist impulses and participatory collective production methods, and dictated by the themes explored in each video, the methods used to make it, the context in which it is produced and to which it responds, and the ways it is distributed and finally seen. Its objectives include education and empowerment, the sharing of information and articulation of an identity; it can be a stage for acts of rebellion or a call to arms; it can serve as evidentiary documentation and bear witness to injustices – that is, it can show what is happening and create a record of what has happened. It has been variously referred to at different times as 'participatory video', 'street video', 'alternative video', 'grassroots media', 'guerrilla television', 'militant video' and 'process video'. Its methods and politics can be seen up to the present day, in 'citizen journalism', 'cyberactivism' and 'anti-extractivist filmmaking' and in some socially engaged art practices.

Video activism has its ideological antecedents in the political filmmaking of the 1930s, notably the newsreels produced by the Federation of Workers Film Societies, and in the radical film collectives of the 1960s, who filmed, distributed and screened their own alternative newsreels outside of and opposed to the dominant narratives of the time.[2] These independent political film groups developed comparable models to those of the video activists who followed after them, while some film collectives would provide space for early video activists to experiment with newly available video technology. Both groups were influenced by similar social and political demands, but their chosen medium and approach differed greatly. Political film groups were largely interested in organising collectively, pooling resources and time to make and show 16mm films with a common goal, with their focus tending to be on local issues and campaigns. Unlike many activist video projects, they were not driven by the imperative to include local communities in the production process. Instead, they placed a greater emphasis on making films about these communities, with individually-named directors and filmmakers expressing their own personal vision.

This particular story of video activism begins in London in 1969, with the arrival of a handful of portable video cameras shared among activists. The movement spread throughout the UK in the 1970s, with the development of numerous community video groups including Sheffield Video Workshop, Community Video Workshop Cardiff, Manchester Film and Video Workshop and Media Workshop Belfast. It further proliferated with the establishment of a number of short-lived cable television channels. The first such station

Familiar Feelings (Common Stock Youth Theatre, 1982).

granted a broadcast licence was Greenwich Cablevision in South-East London in 1972; networks soon followed in Bristol, Sheffield, Swindon, Wellingborough and Milton Keynes. The reach of video expanded again in the 1980s with the establishment of the Workshop Declaration and Channel 4: from 1982 over 50 video workshops were founded. Many of these were expansions of long-running film workshops, such as Birmingham Film and Video Workshop and Amber Films in Newcastle. From the 1990s, with the spread of the worldwide web and ever cheaper and more accessible video recording devices, video activism saw videos of actions and reactions being shared all over the world and began to resemble what we see today.

This book is not an attempt to list all of the activist video projects in the UK; the examples featured here are simply that: examples. Nor does it follow a strict linear chronology; instead, it alternates between decades and themes as the narrative demands. The stories that make up this history are chosen to exemplify the different ways video has been used by activist groups to further their struggles and represent their experiences, as well as to identify some of the through lines of this process.

The production, distribution and exhibition of videos by, from and about misrepresented groups remain in the margins of the history of moving image production in the UK. To focus specifically on video is to draw attention to an area of British moving image history that has been largely overlooked, for three intersecting reasons. First, the relative scarcity of accessible material: the technology of video, alongside activists' focus on process rather than the production of a product, meant that tapes were often recorded over, or else left forgotten, under beds and in attics, subject to decay. Only a small proportion ever made their way into an archive to be preserved or digitised, making it difficult to write about work that is hard to locate, watch or even identify.[3]

Second, the groups responsible for producing activist videos have to date largely been considered parochial amateurs, outside of the film and television industries and their officially-sanctioned television or cinema screens, while at the same time set apart from the networks of avant-garde artist moving image makers and the spaces they occupy and target. Activist video makers have typically been characterised – at least by the kinds of people who tend to write histories – as lacking in the artistic skill and professional know-how to make anything worthy of serious consideration.

Third, the subject matter and aesthetic of activist videos, however urgent and meaningful to the people involved, demonstrates little interest on the part of their makers in the lineage of filmmaking. Activist productions look little like the documentaries and news programmes to which they might otherwise be compared. As a result, little of the work has been deemed historically relevant, and it continues to be hard to classify within recognised genres.

For video activists, the political intention of their work expands beyond the themes and subjects it explores. The process of production and the ways the videos are distributed and exhibited are no less important – and sometimes more so – than the finished videos themselves. Activist videos are often made collaboratively, and for the most part are shared through informal, DIY networks. Instead of established channels and top-down institutions, they are shown in informal screening spaces, often as part of a discussion to elicit an active response from the audience. The early examples of activist video with which this book begins were made in opposition to what the community video practitioner Tony Dowmunt described as 'the late-capitalist status quo', which he understood to be maintained and upheld by the dominant television and documentary modes of the 1970s:

> We believed that for 'the revolution' to succeed, we were all going to have to learn to see things differently, that is to say radical films needed to be made in a radical way.[4]

1 VIDEO HAPPENINGS

Friendships and collaborations were at the centre of London's expanding underground scene in the late 1960s. Here household names including the Beatles and the Rolling Stones rubbed shoulders with self-professed 'dropouts', creating a network of like-minded insiders and outsiders who organised themselves to share the latest information about culture, society, politics and technology. Together they anticipated the needs of their peers and encouraged them to think and work in new and experimental ways. Squatted buildings and ad-hoc spaces provided opportunities for early experiments with video recording technology that were characterised by anti-authoritarianism and interdisciplinarity.

One such place was the Arts Lab, a countercultural hub on Drury Lane in London's Covent Garden. It was co-founded in 1967 by American ex-pat Jack Henry Moore – a self-described 'video freak' and occasional collaborator with Yoko Ono and John Lennon – with his good friend Jim Haynes, whose background was in theatre. The Arts Lab provided an opportunity for different art forms to be pushed up against one another, experimented with and presented anew, challenging conventional modes of making and sharing art. It invited a radical participatory and collaborative approach to production and exhibition; an emphasis on innovations with new technology was central to the programming of events that appealed to outsiders and activists looking for new ways to communicate and create change.

Before the Arts Labs, Jim Haynes had run the Traverse Theatre in Edinburgh and collaborated with Allan Kaprow, who had developed the concept of the 'happening' in New York in the early 1960s. 'Happenings', often combining live performance with lighting, sound and the projection of moving images,

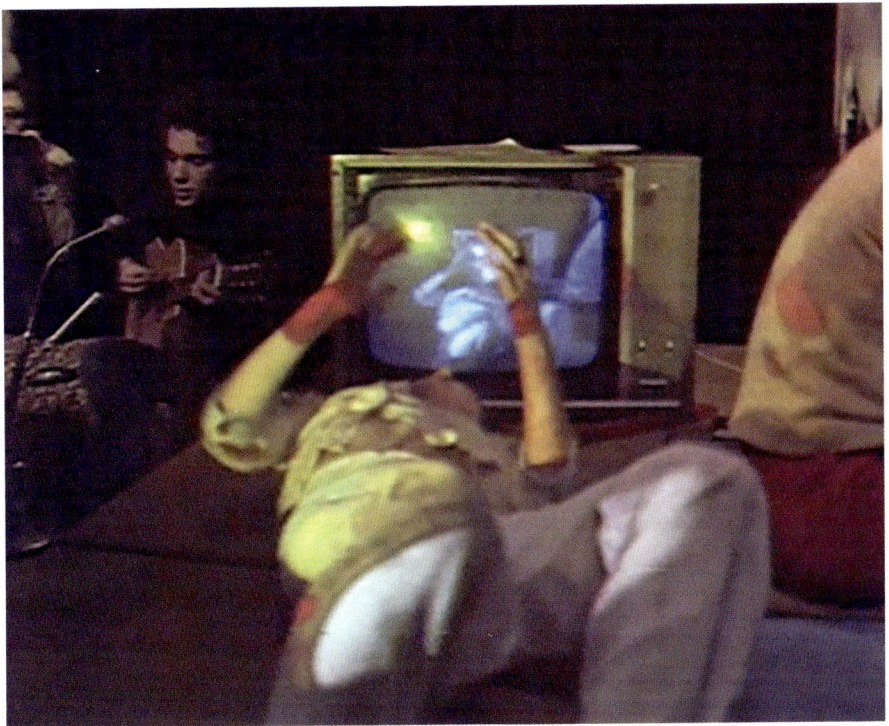

Video Space (John 'Hoppy' Hopkins, 1970).

resulted in films and videos shown in settings other than traditional cinema auditoria: the aim was to create an active audience, one engaged in the production of the art as much as observing it. A 1968 article in the *Observer* newspaper described an encounter with this unorthodox approach to exhibition and participation at the Arts Lab:

> Three films were showing in the basement cinema, where you shed your shoes and recline (since there are no seats) on foam-rubber mattresses ... Images are back-projected on to a vast white sheet – balloons, butterflies, landscapes and townscapes. Dancers appear in silhouette, their outlines synchronised to match the projections ... the sort of art we never see in London nightclubs ... Although I don't relish this kind of participation, I cannot deny its power.[1]

Promoting Arts Lab events (programme, 1968).

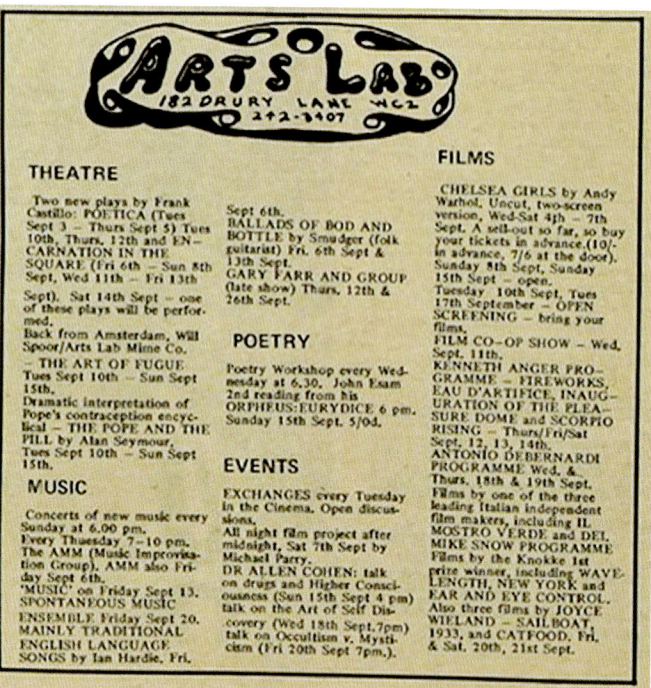

This multi-directional relationship to production and participation would become a defining feature of activist video as the decade progressed.

In the spirit of collaboration, Moore and Haynes were joined by allies including Biddy Peppin and David Curtis, who would later co-found the London Film Makers Co-operative, and David Jeffrey, who designed and built the Arts Lab's cinema and theatre. This auditorium-cum-playground would form the epicentre of an anarchic experiment in the presentation of art and culture, as a 1967 article in the radical underground newspaper the International Times outlined:

> The Laboratory will be centred around a small open space free-form theatre and will contain a space for a rehearsal room which can double as an environment area and serve as a concert hall ... In addition to the theatre they plan to have regular film showings, tape concerts, video tapes, readings, happenings, lectures and exhibitions.[2]

The reference to 'video tapes' as early as 1967, and in the same sentence as more established cultural forms, evidences the interdisciplinary way in which this new technology was already understood. Video was to become one more tool at the artist's disposal, and the role of the artist in turn would expand and unfold.

A report written by the Arts Council seven years later in 1974 notes that the Arts Lab 'attracted a new youthful audience and presented work that otherwise would not have been seen in London,'[3] and reflects on its impact on the subsequent development of alternative arts practices in the UK: by 1969 as many as 50 Arts Labs had been set up around the country, including spaces in Birmingham, Brighton, Exeter, Farnham, Guildford, Huddersfield, Loughborough, Manchester, Southampton and Swindon. The report describes how these spaces provided opportunities for new artistic forms and practices to develop outside the limits of traditional arts institutions and established moving image contexts:

> 'A whole era of youth-oriented activities mushroomed on a scale that London had not seen before ... The organisations were loosely organised and concentrated all their activities towards the encouragement of new work.'[3]

Arts Lab workers.

When the lease for the Drury Lane Arts Lab ran out in 1969 it closed its doors and moved to a new location. In the same year Haynes left London for Paris, and Moore for Amsterdam,[4] but not before they attended an arts festival in Italy, where they had what would be a significant conversation in the story of video activism. At the festival, Haynes and Moore bumped into fellow radical and outsider John 'Hoppy' Hopkins, with whom they had previously collaborated running the London psychedelic club UFO. As Hopkins describes the encounter:

> I hadn't been there for a few days before I ran into Jim Haynes and he mentioned video to me in the course of conversation: As he said it, I knew what it was. I knew that it had been waiting for me. Or I'd been waiting for it. Well it's like a living thing. You get immediate feedback. It completely by-passed all the things that you have to do with film, like setting f-stops and minutely adjusting focus and all that sort of stuff.[5]

Hopkins was well known at the time for his far-reaching involvement in the underground arts and music scene. In the 1960s he had worked as a photojournalist, promoted the rock band Pink Floyd, published the underground newspaper the *International Times* and helped set up the London Free School. On returning to England after the festival, he persuaded Sony to let him borrow an open-reel Portapak so that he could begin to work out how this new technology could be used to support his work in London's alternative underground scene. Hopkins was instantly moved by the potential of video:

> You got instant feedback, you could see what you were getting and video tape, although it was relatively expensive, it was basically cheap, and of course you could use it again and again. And it moved being a photographer mainly working in black-and-white, well you could do all of the same things but the pictures moved. I was struck, and stayed struck for about the next twenty years.[6]

The earliest recorded activist video in the UK was made two months later, in April 1969, when Hopkins documented a housing demonstration and a street theatre performance. Shot on two-inch tape using a Sony CV-2100, one of the first portable video cameras, the video is labelled 'Notting Hill demo (first tape ever shot)'. It was a particularly significant tape for Hopkins because 'it was the first one, there were no rules at all'.[7] The use of video in this context is indicative of the way the new technology would continue to be mobilised, and the novelty of its use gleaned a short article in *Time Out* magazine, making reference to the unique specificity of instant playback at the time:

> 'Mobile Video Unit: If you happen to see a screen showing a film of an event you were involved in the previous day, then you will have fallen victim of John Hopkins' experiment in television reportage.'[8]

Notting Hill demo consists of long, meandering, handheld shots, recorded from the point of view of crowds of young people out in the streets, jostling with uniformed policemen while passers-by look on with a mixture of

John 'Hoppy' Hopkins.

support and irritation. The footage, edited in-camera, is broken up by a flickering, horizontal fuzz and the audible click of the stop and record buttons being pressed. The soundtrack comprises a live, synched voiceover from Hopkins describing what was being recorded, along with the shouts, chants and jeers commonly heard at demonstrations.

In a move to legitimise and fund his experiments with video, later that year Hopkins successfully applied to the newly formed New Activities Committee at the Arts Council for financial support to record more videos. In his application letter he relates that he had been borrowing a camera from John Lennon to make a visual record of local events, and makes no mention of the loan from Sony. It's possible, of course, that Hopkins used a number of different video cameras during this time – or perhaps he thought name-dropping a Beatle might help his case. London's burgeoning underground scene benefited from a similar gift: when the early American video camera brand Ampex brought out its own one-inch Video Tape Recorders in the late 1960s, in a bid to encourage their creative use the company gave one to each of the four members of the Beatles. But John, Ringo and George didn't know what to do with their gifts, so they gave them to Hopkins.[9] Following his early period of experimentation, Hopkins began to see video as a 'generalised tool, which could be used by various people for various means.' These 'use categories', as he called them, included the arts, pop music, TV companies, news reportage, filmmaking and local TV.[10]

By the end of 1969, it was time for video to take up more than just a supporting role. After the closure of the original Arts Lab, the New Arts Lab, also known as the Institute for Research and Technology (IRAT), was established in North London. It took up residence in a four-storey factory building rented by Camden Council to a number of the original Arts Labs members, along with a growing cohort of new collaborators, including Hopkins. IRAT built on the Arts Labs' interdisciplinary nature, with a focus on combining art and technology including 'Cinema, electronics, cybernetics, exhibitions, music, photographics, printing, music, theatre, video, words, semiotics, the Computer Arts society, London Film-makers Co-op...'[11] As with Hopkins's wide-ranging 'use categories', the diversity of disciplines from which this group of about 25 people were drawn highlights just how widely the new technology was already being recognised and explored, and illustrates the context for the growing use of video by activists.

Under the guidance of Hopkins and friends, IRAT housed not one but two dedicated video workshops, which aimed to find new audiences and settings for their experiments with video. TVX was 'the reckless experimental group', which sought to make and screen videos in spaces outside of and opposed to established institutions. The Centre for Advanced TV Studies (CATS), through a combination of research and publishing, was more respectable, engaging with organisations such as the Institute of Mass Communications Research, as well as colleges and universities. It was under the auspices of these new workshops that Hopkins' work with video began to be recognised and understood by larger organisations.

In 1970, members of TVX received an unexpected invitation from the BBC to present some of their experiments with video on television. The idea was for TVX to build on its previous experience producing happenings at the Arts Lab and organise and record something similar in one of the BBC's studios. TVX members saw this as a chance to infiltrate the hallowed space of broadcast television on their own terms. Together, they produced an 18-minute piece titled *Video Space* (1970), which combined Super-8 film,

The New Arts Lab's sliding red doors, Robert Street, London.

'Yippies' invade *The Frost Programme* (ITV, tx 7/11/1970).

16mm film and 2-inch video with a light show, a dancer and some musicians. This was brought together with elements of live and recorded dialogue. It was, recalled Hopkins,

> something that no one had seen before, especially on this side of the Atlantic, which was a way to try and use the medium of broadcast TV ... in a way which conformed more to art than to documentary or conventional programming.'[12]

Due to disagreements between the BBC and TVX, *Video Space* was never broadcast, but it did lead to the commissioning of a number of shorter pieces by TVX, that were made and broadcast on the BBC in October 1970.[13] The final video piece TVX made for television was called *Do You Love Me*: three minutes long, recorded on 2-inch video and described as a 'Visualisation of a track by Frank Zappa and Band'.[14] Its inclusion of imagery referencing the anti-racist activists the White Panthers drew a complaint from the influential 'clean-up TV' campaigner Mary Whitehouse. Subsequently, the BBC terminated TVX's contract.

Hopkins has since reflected, with some regret, on the shortlived relationship between TVX and broadcast television. In doing so, he draws attention to the compromises that would have been necessary in order to be accepted by more legitimate, larger organisations:

> We were rather brash and I think rather stupid at the time, because there was the possibility of opening that crack in the wall of the establishment, to get more high-quality broadcast TV done from an artistic basis, and I think in retrospect if we'd behaved differently and not so aggressively, we might have got further with the BBC.[15]

It wasn't only disagreements with the BBC; just a month later there was a further clash of ideologies between another member of TVX and a TV broadcaster. On 7 November 1970, during a live edition of ITV's *The Frost Programme*, an interview with the American social activist Jerry Rubin of the Youth International Party, popularly known as the 'Yippies', was disrupted by members of the studio audience, who occupied the stage and invited others to join them in front of the cameras. They proceeded to pass around what looked like a joint, and heckled the audience, the programme crew and presenter David Frost. TVX member John Kirk was one of the invaders, and video-recorded the entire episode with a Sony Portapak. Foreshadowing the demands and actions of later video activists, the camera moves from the viewpoint of the audience, recording the action on stage, to take up a space in front of the studio cameras, turning the video camera back onto them.[16] The group later wrote about their motivations for the invasion in the alternative newspaper *Friends*. Their demands, bolstered by their newfound access to video recording technology, highlight the inequality of access to forms of representation at the time:

> Our interests and life-style are being misrepresented both in media and in Government ... We are people who know what we want and we will disrupt any attempt to block or misrepresent our views. What we want is media time

proportional to our population density, to use the way we decide. Time in the TV studios open to any group wishing to participate. If there aren't enough stations with enough time, amend the broadcastings acts to allow for the setting up of local community TV stations using both cable and broadcast ...[17]

For TVX, the invasion only created a momentary disruption; the monolith of normal programming remained, challenged but unchanged, at least for the time being.

Ultimately, it was through the work of CATV that video would gain wider recognition, not as a supplement to broadcast television, but as a social and political tool. In 1971, Hopkins was commissioned by the University of Southampton to carry out some research for the Home Office about the use of video in community development. With the small amount of research money available, Hopkins visited North America, where the use of video by activist and community groups was more established. In New York, he spent time with a number of independent videomakers, including the Raindance Corporation and the Alternate Media Centre, who were already developing video projects in support of social and political aims. In Montreal he met with videomakers involved in the hugely influential Challenge for Change project, established in 1966 by the National Film Board of Canada to pioneer the use of video in communities. Hopkins recalled that he 'picked up a lot of ideas, both artistic and social, from that visit'.[18]

Hopkins' findings appeared in the 1972 publication *Video in Community Development*.[19] Featuring case studies and articles on activist video projects developed in Australia, as well as North America, the pamphlet describes how grassroots groups and video practitioners in the UK could use these processes.[20] Much of the video work covered in the publication had advantages over projects that were being initiated in the UK, notably support from state funding, distribution via established cable television networks and prolonged access to portable video recording equipment. All the same, the pamphlet's practical and technical advice on the use of portable video technology made it an invaluable resource, enabling video practitioners in the UK to begin to conceptualise their work in a broader international context.

In the three years since the arrival of the portable video camera onto to London's burgeoning underground scene, this new technology had slipped from the clutches of television studios and home video enthusiasts into the hands of experimental artists and activists. Freed from the restrictions of broadcast television, video would go on to be used to oppose and critique it, either directly or indirectly, through its application in social and political contexts influenced by its use in North America. With these new innovations would come new aesthetics that centred the experiences of the people in front of and behind the camera, very much reflecting the interdisciplinary context in which video was being used and shared. As the 1960s drew to a close and the Beatles broke up, the 1970s ushered in a new period of political upheaval. Video provided a means for those most impacted to invent their own modes of communication and fairer forms of representation, outside of and in opposition to the mainstream. Once they had seen themselves on that flickering box in the corner there was no going back. Their sights were set on TV – and it would never look the same again.

Close-up: The Sony Portapak

The portable video tape recorders made by Sony in Japan were the most widely used models in the UK in the early 1970s. Other companies developing similar technology at the same time were Panasonic and Akai, also in Japan, and Ampex in the USA. Following the successful launch of its first 'pocket-sized' portable transistor radio in 1958, Sony set about adapting large and unwieldy broadcast video technology with a view to developing portable video recording equipment.

At this point, video was firmly in the hands of television studios and accessible only to media professionals. Early television video recording employed a clunky 'Quadruplex' or transverse system. The machinery was the size of two washing machines and used four large magnetic heads to vertically scan two-inch tape at a 90-degree angle to simultaneously record and reproduce images and sounds.

Between 1964 and 1969, in its quest for portability, Sony began to develop helical two-head technology that recorded diagonally onto half-inch tape. This allowed the tape to carry the same amount of information as a Quadruplex tape, but at a quarter of the width. Fewer heads and narrower tape made possible a much more compact and portable unit, closer in size to a large, over-the-shoulder handbag.

In 1964, Sony unveiled the CV-2000, a helical-scan, monochrome, open-reel video recorder with attachable camera, microphone and monitor. It was the company's first step towards the creation of a video tape recorder for home use in both size and cost. The recording unit itself weighed 20kg, was the size of a small suitcase and, with the video camera attachment, cost US$1,425 (roughly US$11,000 today).

Over the next five years, Sony released five more models in the CV range, each advancing image and sound capabilities while reducing size and cost. In 1967, the

An introduction to working with video, from publication *Basic Video in Community Work* (1975).

company released the fifth and final CV model, the CV-2400, also known as the Video Rover and later referred to as the Portapak. It was made up of two parts – the handheld video camera (weighing around 2.5kg); and a half-inch reel-to-reel tape recorder (just under 5kg without the battery pack) – and could record up to 20 minutes of black-and-white video footage.

The term 'Portapak' was used in promotional materials and taken up as shorthand by its users to stress the compact portability that was its most compelling feature. Print advertising showed the recording unit and camera being worn by models with ease, over one shoulder. Sony's 1970 annual report heralds three imminent new models, including 'a model offering both color and black-and-white recording, a model offering fully automatic recording and a battery-powered completely compact model'.[21]

Despite rapid advances in portable video camera technology, the video cameras used by activist groups were still quite primitive. The first playback decks many activists got their hands on had heavy battery packs, which limited their portablity, and offered only rudimentary fast-forward and rewind capabilities. Much early work with video was transmitted from camera to monitor or from camera to camera. Screening pre-recorded information required a playback deck, which was either connected to an ordinary television through the antenna terminals of the set, or else presented on monitors, which had the same horizontal flicker as television.

Because of this mode of presentation, video was an audiovisual language that resembled the monolithic, one-directional mode of television, but one in which – crucially to this story – the control of the content lay in the hands of the users.

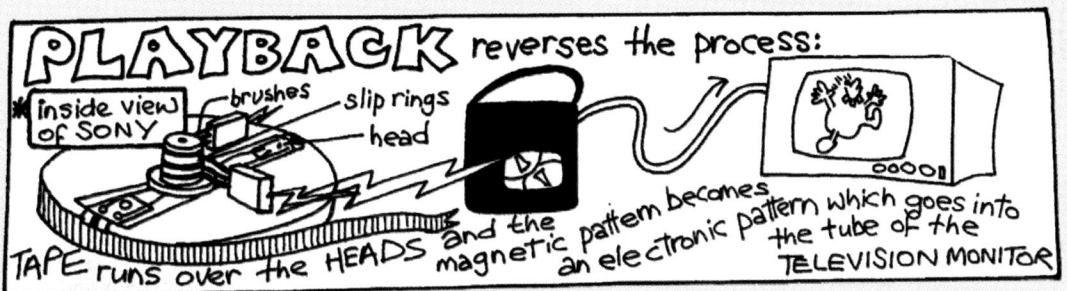

2. SEE YOURSELF ON TV!

In early 1977, flyers began to appear on walls and lampposts around West London. In hand-drawn, blocky, purple text, silkscreened on off-white A4 sheets, they read, 'EVER BEEN ON TV? YOU COULD BE – THIS WEEK.' The flyers invited local residents to take part in an experiment in producing their own news programmes. The project, established by West London Media Workshop (WLMW), aimed to counter the exclusion of residents from their own representation by creating a two-way exchange of information – one which would for the first time allow them to see themselves 'on TV' on their own terms.

'At that time,' noted Andy Porter, one of the project's founders, 'people didn't see themselves on any kind of TV.' With an instinct that is emblematic of those involved in activist video projects, Porter wanted to know what would happen if they 'put the control of media in the hands of those it was seeking to represent'.[1] Having already established a community-run newspaper and a local photographic darkroom, Porter and WLMW's four other co-founders had begun to wonder how activist video production could benefit existing community groups and support local forms of activism. Following a series of small-scale, community-led video projects, they initiated a local news service called, 'News at West 10' (W10 being the postcode of the area where the project was based).

The proliferation of video cameras in the 1970s meant that activists and community groups in the UK who wanted to make and distribute their own version of television could load their monitors and video playback decks into cars, trolleys or old prams to screen videos in playgrounds, launderettes, libraries,

News at W.10 flyer, 1977.

crèches and on street corners. For WLMW, the joint aim was to communicate and possibly resolve neighbourhood issues, while stimulating community and audience involvement, both in front of and behind the camera. It was their hope that a locally-made video news service could lead to an open discussion about the neighbourhood and build solidarity between isolated residents.

Over a six-month period between 1976 and 1977, *News at West 10* produced four tapes, each lasting between ten and 20 minutes and covering issues and activities relevant to the neighbourhood.[2] Topics included cuts to the borough's public services, the lack of support for childminders, the opening of a drop-in club for mothers with new babies and a strike following the sacking of a local children's play worker. Sadly, none of the videos have survived. All that remains are a written report and a handful of still images, from which we can glean that the programmes mimicked the form of broadcast news, with presenters addressing the audience or interviewing people on the streets, collecting opinions and activating discussions. But in contrast to what the tapes' audiences saw every evening on their TVs at home, the subjects looked and sounded like them, while the footage was handheld and shaky, with the sound quality dependent on how windy it was and how close the microphone was to the speaker.

Local screening events, at which participants and their neighbours watched the videos played back on monitors, were as integral to the project as the production of the videos themselves. The variety of venues that were selected for playback – pensioners' clubs, adventure playgrounds, a health centre, shopping precincts and church halls – highlight the potential for such projects to bring different audiences into contact with one another. The finished videos were replayed from the back of a van or from a monitor wheeled around in a converted pram.

The report, *Community Media: Community Communication in the UK*, published in 1980, highlighted the opportunities that localised production and distribution methods opened up:

> ... it begins to develop new communications processes in society, releasing information from new sources in a variety of directions; it frees the medium for use as a tool for exchanging ideas, explaining the world, for dialogue in an open and direct way.[3]

News at West 10 playback at St Thomas Church Hall, Kensal Town.

While the reach of these videos was limited by geography, the audiences, who were often also involved in the production in front of and behind the camera, were able to see one another represented on the small screen. In contrast to cinematic projection, the modest-sized monitor brought an intimacy and connection between screen and audience, akin to their relationship with broadcast television but with a radically different subject matter and point of view. The report continues:

> The size of the television image is such that it presents people and situations usually at less than life size. This means that the person viewing is much more in charge of what he/she is seeing, the television invites reaction, rather than forces reaction. Because the audio-visual stimulation is low-key, he/she is less likely to be overwhelmed, the experience is containable and therefore more open to be shared, discussed, used collectively ... Everything works to make it part of what is going on, rather than the absolute dictator. People can see each other, exchange eye contact, talk while the programme is going on; it is an experience that is collective and mutual and can create the conditions for follow up discussions and interaction.[4]

News at West 10 van screening at Kensal Shopping Precinct.

As the 1970s progressed, broadcasters created opportunities for activists to access television, though with fewer resources and greater restrictions than those offered to professional TV producers. These offers took two forms: those activists who wanted their fair share of representation on the airwaves were invited into the studios, as long as they adopted the terms set by the broadcaster, or else they were provided with infrastructure similar to broadcast television, but without comparable resources or reach. These two new initiatives, both established in 1972, advocated for different forms of 'citizen's television' that embodied the ideals of access and participation made possible by portable video recording technology. The Community Programme Unit (CPU) was founded as part of BBC Two's public service remit to provide community programming on the BBC. Meanwhile, the Conservative government granted licences to a number of local cable television networks.

The CPU's approach to production and programming was intended to provide a counter to traditional programme structures and their aesthetically homogenous programming. The BBC's then director of programming, David Attenborough – now better known for his work in front of the camera – hoped that activists and video pioneers would bring with them 'voices, attitudes and opinions, that, for one reason or another have been unheard or seriously neglected by mainstream programmes' As well as the following ambitious aims:

> Stylistic innovations, new ways of handling film or video tape which professional broadcasters have either ignored or rejected; new editorial attitudes that do not derive from the assumptions of the university educated elite who are commonly believed to dominate television production.[5]

This was perhaps a tall order when the allocated slot was at 11.30pm, one evening a week. The CPU was founded on the basis of ongoing conversations about increasing access so that a more diverse range of people and experiences could be seen on screen, and was modelled on early ideas and approaches to activist video production. Attenborough expanded on this proposition:

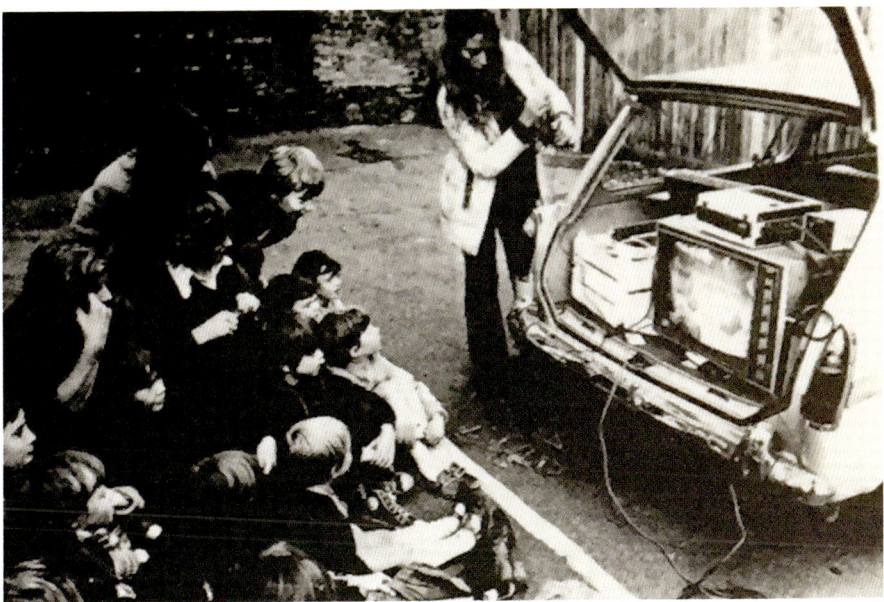

Inter-Action playback, from *Basic Video in Community Work* (1975).

'Access' or 'community programmes', which are spoken of so frequently in the current debates about broadcasting, are taken to be programmes which are made by viewers who have applied for airtime, and for which professional broadcasters supply the technical facilities necessary for production and transmission, but play only a minimal part in editorial decisions.[6]

Ten new programmes were made as part of BBC Two's newly-launched *Open Door* strand, described in the *Radio Times* as a slot 'where people and groups are given a chance to have their own say, in their own way.'[7]

The CPU approached potential groups and received applications to make a programme. Successful applicants were then allotted a producer and assistant as well as the use of the research capabilities of the BBC. Editorial control was enabled for the 'accessee' through every stage of production, from planning and scripting to filming and editing.[8] Initially, programmes made for *Open Door* were live studio broadcasts. Later they would also embrace on-location and pre-recorded material. Each programme was approximately 30 minutes in length and was broadcast in colour; the shaky black-and-white video footage associated with activist videos at the time was replaced with crisp imagery and clear sound. The form and aesthetic were dictated by the theme or subject matter being explored in the programme, and included fly-on-the-wall documentation of various everyday and not-so-everyday activities, talking heads, vox pops and group discussions.

Early episodes featured a group of Black teachers discussing the effect of the English education system on Black children (tx. 16/4/1973), the Transex Liberation Group (tx. 4/6/1973) presenting a frank and open discussion around 'transsexualism', the Bootstrap Union (tx. 15/10/1973), a group of teachers and parents, debating problems in schools in deprived areas, and a meeting of the Gypsy Council (tx. 3/12/1973) with friends and non-sympathisers for discussion, ceremonies, songs and dancing. The list of programmes and topics covered stand as a testament to what public access broadcasting could look like. Each programme attempted to represent the position or point of view of a specific community group, exploring issues relating to identity or social politics – some more successfully than others.

In 1979, *Open Door* broadcast 'It Ain't Half Racist Mum' (tx. 1/3/1979), made with the Campaign against Racism in the Media and presented by

Three editions of the BBC's *Open Door* (top to bottom): 'Starting to Happen' (1974), 'Black Teachers Group' (1973), 'Transex Liberation Group' (1973).

Stuart Hall and Maggie Steed. The programme took the form of a newscast in which Hall and Steed took turns to use clips taken from popular sitcoms and news programmes of the day to highlight and critique the ways in which broadcast television upheld and cultivated racist viewpoints. Disappointingly – and revealingly in terms of *Open Door*'s limitations – the BBC chose not to address the inherent bias and racism to which the programme drew attention, taking it as a cue to instigate structural change, but instead elected to apologise to the actors and presenters included in the programme as part of Hall and Steed's critique.

In an effort to demonstrate the *open* nature of *Open Door*, many episodes were bookended with a group discussion involving those who participated in the production of the programme – much like the discussions that would take place after a community video screening. These conversations were an attempt to frame the participants as actively engaged in how they were represented. The context of the television studio, however, often worked against this. With a presenter and a fixed panel, the discussions did nothing to destabilise the pre-existing hierarchies of broadcast television. With little opportunity for critical feedback, these moments ended up replicating the rigidity and formality of typical BBC programming. Once they entered the sacred space of the television studio, participants found they were unable to represent themselves on their own terms and instead had to rely on a format set by the broadcaster. Many of the community groups involved in *Open Door* felt thrust into a televisual ghetto, unwillingly complicit in a pervasively undemocratic and misrepresentative system. A 1990 article illustrates the tension felt at the time between the board at the BBC and the CPU staff:

> The BBC Board of Governors besieged Attenborough claiming producers were a guerrilla unit using the BBC to promote their own left-wing ideology. Critics from the left denounced the project as a plot to make the BBC more legitimate, attacking even those groups who were given access.[9]

One of the defining characteristics of activist video projects was the participants' control over the presentation of their videos, but it became clear that engaging with such monolithic and controlling institutions undermined much of the liberatory potential of activist and community-led video projects.¹⁰ The BBC's production processes and programme structures couldn't – or wouldn't – yield to the specific needs and experiences of the community groups they sought to engage.

In parallel with the BBC's Community Programmes Unit, from 1972 the Conservative government offered up six 'experimental' licences for local cable television stations, which would provide opportunities for underrepresented groups and individuals to develop and broadcast their own TV programmes. The offer of locally-made programming initially appeared out of step with the top-down control more commonly associated with the government at the time. The television industry decided to support the scheme – despite uncertainty as to how it might be financially beneficial, since neither subscription nor advertising were permitted. Rather the 'experiment' was to be, in part, a test case as to whether, in time, a subscriber model could be established.

The first station granted a licence was Greenwich Cablevision in South-East London. Rediffusion's Bristol Channel came next in May 1973; British Relay began programming on its Sheffield network in August 1973; the following month Swindon Viewpoint was launched, with EMI financing Radio Rental's local network. Wellingborough Cablevision started in March 1974. Milton Keynes's Channel 40 came later in December 1976.¹¹ This mode of video

Camerawoman, Sheffield Cablevision.

production was significant in the story of video activism as it provided the largest financial support for participatory and community-led video production; 'more money was spent on them than any other sphere of low-gauge video activity – approximately £100,000 between 1972 and 1978.'[12]

Milton Keynes was one of a number of new towns built in the late 1960s and early 1970s outside of London, as part of a government-driven programme to relieve pressure on housing. The cable network was one of the features of this modern, forward-looking development. An introductory leaflet published by Channel 40, the town's new network, gives a sense of what the new stations were hoping to achieve:

> ... [this is] the first time in the UK that an experiment in community use of cable television has been set up on an entirely independent and non-commercial basis. Starting in December 1976 we will be transmitting to all new city homes a few hours each week of locally produced programmes made by, with and for people living in Milton Keynes.[13]

Set up by British Telecom with the Milton Keynes Development Corporation in 1976, Channel 40 was run out of a building on one of the town's housing estates. The launch leaflet concludes by describing the aims of the new channel: to serve the people of the city by providing them with a means to access information about Milton Keynes and, in the spirit of early video activism, 'access to a means of expression, to enable individuals and groups in Milton Keynes to share their interests and points of view with others'.[14] Unfortunately, the people in charge at Channel 40 soon found out that enabling access to the means of production was not, in itself, enough to engage the local community in producing their own television. It proved difficult to meet the expectations of participants, and problems arose from attempts to redirect and distribute the potential participatory power of this new medium. A 1980 report on the impact and development of cable television notes that 'these attitudes were very much dictated by who was put in day-to-day charge of running the individual stations,'[15] and identified a pattern of internal conflicts, particularly 'to do with the workers, either individually or collectively, wishing to democratise the television service more and the management resisting these developments.'¹⁶ Channel 40 reached an early impasse when, after a reckoning with an onslaught of pigeon fanciers and hobbyists vying for the airwaves, managers realised that their build-it-and-they-will-come policy was not gleaning the results they had hoped for.

In 1977, Channel 40 hired Carry Gorney, a community artist and activist specialising in video, to try and meet the aims of the network *and* respond to the needs of local residents. Gorney had previously developed video projects based around play, drama and youth work with groups at the London-based community arts organisation Inter-Action, and hoped to try something similar in Milton Keynes. Cable television lacked the resources and reach provided by the BBC to the *Open Door* participants, but it did provide Gorney with a structure similar to broadcast television, though with greater freedom and fewer limitations. From the start, she observed an imbalance between the network's proposal and the reality of its operation: 'I had a lot of arguments with people at Channel 40 because their policy was open door, which meant that anybody could come in, pick up a camera and make a programme.'¹⁷

Gorney was already active in the women's movement, regularly attending meetings and groups for women with similar interests. Noting that many early video experiments were dominated by men, she saw an opportunity at Channel 40 to combine her political interests with her video work, and set out to collaborate with a group of disparate and isolated women, mainly wives and mothers, who had just arrived in Milton Keynes to live on the newly-built housing estates. Like Gorney's women's meetings, the video project provided an opportunity for the participants to share their knowledge and experiences with one another and subsequently to use video to produce a series of information and discussion programmes intended to extend and further share this process:

> I was interested in the group work and issues of social isolation and the kind of dilemmas the women on the estates were facing; that began to engage me and involve me totally ... [I] thought what we ought to do is to set up groups on the estates, let's use video as a tool for doing that, let's use Channel 40 as a vehicle for communicating some of the ideas and thoughts that women had, and create a network of women.¹⁸

Greenwich Cablevision shop.

To determine the subjects that would be covered in the videos, the participants adapted consciousness-raising methodologies developed by the contemporary women's movement, whereby the personal accounts and experiences of those involved became the basis for group discussions. Rather than relying on an interviewer or director, the women shared responsibilities and were able to collapse the traditional roles and hierarchies of interrogation and manipulation associated with didactic and dogmatic approaches to making television.

Over the space of a month in February 1979, 16 different programmes, under the series title *Things that Mother Never Told Us!*, were broadcast into the houses of Milton Keynes. Facilitated by Gorney and developed by the women she met through the project, the videos explored themes ranging from childcare and education to socializing, personal relationships, family and friendship. One programme, simply called 'Women Talking', featured a group of women discussing problems around marriage openly and spontaneously. The series also took advantage of live phone-ins to further involve

Swindon Cable edit suite.

the audience in the content and direction of the programming. It adopted a magazine format, with hosts initiating discussions and to-camera segues leading onto location documentary footage of women going about their daily lives in their own and each other's homes, at the shops, in schools and in care roles. The interviewer and camera equipment are often in shot and their questions back and forth are unedited, allowing discussions to develop and shift, using familiar language and colloquial dialect.

Over the course of the project 150 women took part, from initiating groups or getting involved in discussions, through to filming and editing, which was carried out collaboratively by the participants; all of this helped the production remain open and reflective. Although staff at Channel 40 gave a considerable amount of technical assistance to the women making the tapes, the ideas and topics discussed were based on the experiences and concerns of the women themselves. *Things That Mother Never Told Us!* took the 'personal is political' ethos of the women's movement out of the living rooms of isolated women and onto the television screens of Milton Keynes.

The programmes the women made together highlight the way early activist video projects centred group discussions rather than individualised 'talking heads'; they also provided a space to influence and explore the isolation and misrepresentation experienced by the participants involved in their production. This approach collapsed the divide between the subject and the filmmaker, challenging conventional ideas around accountability and consent. Unfortunately, but perhaps unsurprisingly, *Things that Mother Never Told Us!* proved to be an anomaly. It soon became clear that the priorities of the new cable television stations were largely antithetical to those of activist video groups. Although their stated aim was to provide community-led, democratic control of the airwaves by 'the people', the channels were increasingly run like businesses, with a focus on trying to make money through the sale of advertising slots to local enterprises. As each of these new experiments in access developed, the co-opting of video activism by top-down organisations provided a driver for a shift away from a disruptive and oppositional approach to collective video production and towards something compromising and largely unsatisfying for video activists, as community artist Su Braden recalled:

> In 1976, those who make use of access television, far from enjoying the anonymity of technical production, are guided to make programmes look as much as possible like their 'professional' counterparts. There is no thought of simplifying the technology to enable participants to have fuller control of the form of their contribution.[19]

From the outside, these new stations seemed to be in alignment with the aims of video activism: certainly, they presented voices and experiences rarely seen on television. However, this commitment to freeing up the airwaves for anyone wielding a video camera proved short-lived, and soon became bound up in wider governmental policies relating to the commercialisation and regulation of the airwaves. In contrast to the rigidity and bureaucracy of editorial boards and the control by committee that pervaded the BBC, the new cable television stations suffered from a lack of structure and support. In March 1975, Bristol Channel, not yet two years old, became the first of the cable TV

Opposite page: Carry Gorney with a playback deck in Milton Keynes.

Making the *Things That Mother Never Told Us!* series (Carry Gorney, Inter-Action/Channel 40, 1979).

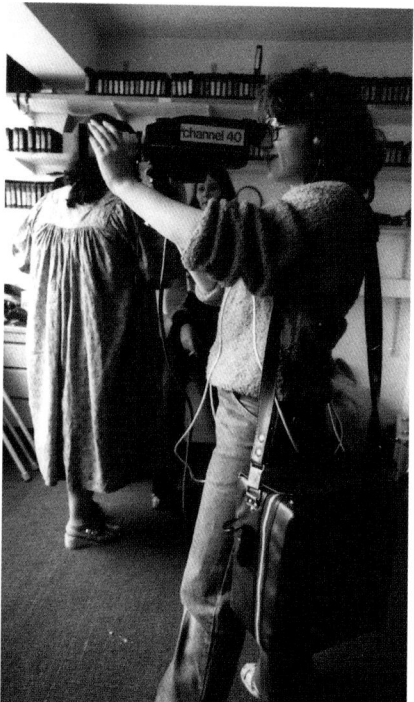

stations to be forced to close its doors. Volunteers were able to salvage 100 tapes (which were later donated to the BFI National Archive) and six portapaks, which were taken up by the newly formed Avon Community Communications Association. The Sheffield and Wellingborough stations closed later that same year. Swindon Viewpoint, acquired by a community group for £1, was able to continue network transmissions for several years, with a community video group continuing to the present day.[20] Their disappointing experiences with community broadcasters convinced many activists of the need to think differently and develop their own forms and modes of self-representation and distribution. As the 1970s drew to a close, advances in home video meant that alternative TV and activist video projects, liberated from the constraints of top-down broadcast television and the fleeting promises of cable television, were able to experiment and to continue to respond to the specific politics and needs of the communities of which they were part.

Throughout the 1980s, home video revolutionised both the consumption and production of moving images. By the middle of the decade, domestic video recording and playback technology had become much more widespread (and much more portable), and now offered an unprecedented platform for the distribution of alternative and activist video material. According to the 'Video Active Report', a 1985 survey of independent video production, by the mid-1980s 35 to 45 per cent of households in Britain had video recorders; 'put simply, people are much more aware of the way they can use video, whether that is for recreation, education or campaigning'.[21]

In 1982 the video co-op Despite TV was established by Mark Saunders as part of Tower Hamlets Arts Project[22] in Whitechapel, east London. Taking advantage of new colour video cameras and the now-dominant VHS (Video Home System) technology, Despite TV produced and distributed one half-hour colour DIY 'TV' project roughly every two months between 1982 and 1983. The videos, made by, for and about the local neighbourhood, covered such themes as changes to health and social services, local education initiatives, housing struggles, gentrification and unemployment. Much like *Things That Mother Never Told Us!*, each edition adopted a magazine approach, allowing for a multiplicity of voices and stories to be shared. Instead of having a host connecting each segment, they were butted up against one another, evoking the experience of 'channel-hopping'. The first edition opened with a segment on local cuts to health services and went on to include an item on the Greater London Council and another made by a local youth group, followed by live footage of a local band, the Mint Juleps.[23] Unlike previous activist video projects, such as West London Media Workshop, which tended to have a core team overseeing every aspect of the production, Saunders was keen to avoid having the video resources tightly controlled by a few salaried individuals. Instead, to maximise individual input, he collectivised the equipment, allowing anyone to author their own contribution to the magazine.

Initially, Despite TV screened their videos in venues similar to those used by WLMW, but by the 1980s simple, low-cost video reproduction and widespread access to VCRs made possible less resource-intensive distribution models. They began sharing their videos though a community bookshop and established a video lending library as well as a mail order service; local libraries were also persuaded to distribute their tapes. The Video Active report details their innovative distribution model:

> They researched where VCRs were located in possible venues, including pubs, clubs, old people's drop-in centres and youth clubs. The tapes were then distributed by them to these venues, left for an agreed period, usually a week, then collected and passed on to another venue.[24]

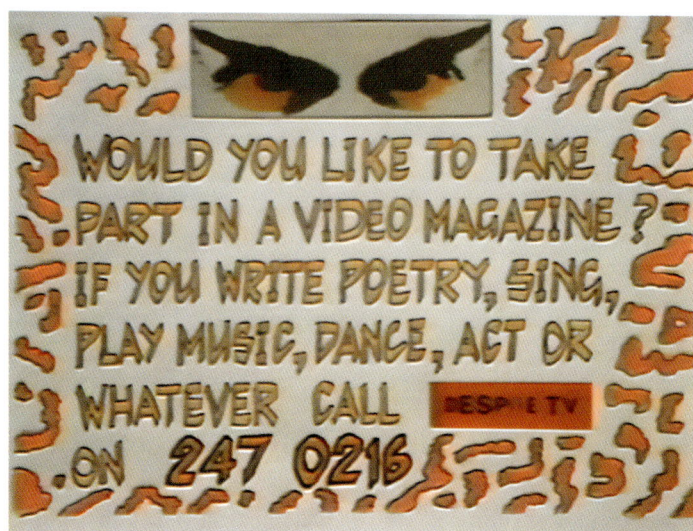

Despite TV (1984).

Despite TV 1 (1983).

This meant that multiple copies of the same video would be circulating in the borough at any one time.

From the moment they got their hands on video cameras and saw footage they had shot and starred in flickering on playback monitors, activists had begun to experiment with making their own television productions. They adopted and adapted what was being fed to them by broadcasters to develop forms of hyper-local television. Noting growing demands for self-repesentation, senior figures in government and broadcasting looked for a means to accommodate them – while carefully ensuring nothing threatened the status quo. For video activists, the price of entering the studios of either the BBC or the local cable television networks was to blunt or abandon the politics that was central to their practice.

In the face of such obstacles, video activists opted to reject compromise. Instead they would continue to challenge the mainstream media's exclusion and misrepresentation of marginalised groups and experiences, developing new models for what would follow.[25]

Close-up: Community Arts and the Basement Project

The politics and practices of what we now know as UK video activism started out as community video, which developed alongside the 1970s community arts movement. The movement included playwrights and actors making street theatre performances and forming groups such as Half Moon in East London and The Blackie in Liverpool; filmmakers and photographers establishing community workshops such as Amber Film & Photography Collective in Newcastle and Blackfriars Photography Project in South London; and writers and artists transferring their practice to public spaces with self-publishing and mural projects by organisations such as Freeform and Centerprise in East London.

The Basement Project was set up in London's East End in the early 1970s, growing out of a demand by local groups for arts activities including drama, music, poetry, photography, woodwork and screen printing. There was also a film and video group, led largely by filmmaker Maggie Pinhorn. That group's first film was *Tunde's Film* (1973), made by, for and from the experience of local working-class young people. Co-directed by and starring Tunde Ikoli, one of the young people from the Project, it offers a social-realist portrait of a racially-mixed group of friends struggling to find work on the streets of Tower Hamlets. Skint and harassed by the police, the boys decide to try to rob a bank. Although shot on film, this project was later used as a trigger for young people to produce their own videos, and the process used to develop it pre-figured the more speculative, performance-centred activist video projects that emerged in the 1980s.

These early community arts groups provided a context for their work to liberate, affect change and create new forms of self-representation for marginalised groups. Reflecting on *Tunde's Film* and her later work with video, Pinhorn remarked:

> Reality is the most important feature. Then to fantasise on that reality. What might be and what could happen. Everything is bound totally within people's own terms of reference. The streets they live in, the flats they inhabit, those are their stories.[26]

By 1978, over half of the 178 community arts projects in the UK were using video.[27] A 1974 Arts Council report offers a useful survey – as well as a means to frame the origins of activist video in the UK:

Tunde's Film
(Maggie Pinhorn/
Tunde Ikoli, 1973).

> The key element in this picture is an individual or group of individuals, perhaps best describable as *animateurs*. They are likely to form themselves into an organization with a name and sometimes even with a constitution ... To a greater or lesser degree they carry their work into the environment of the community itself – streets, pubs, etc. What matters most is the commitment and dedication of the individuals involved ... Their primary aim is to bring about change – psychological, social or political – in a community.[28]

Community art was characterised by three interdependent components, which it shared with community video and which set a precedent for what would become activist video. First, practitioners began to work outside of galleries, moving onto the streets, into community centres or self-organised and collectively-run spaces, often located in temporarily occupied buildings. This in turn encouraged a multimedia, multi-disciplinary approach, where different ways of making and sharing work brushed up against one another, dissolving the boundary between the audience, the maker and what was being made. Second, new forms of expression emerged, specific to the needs of marginalised and under-represented groups. Finally, and perhaps most significantly for video activism, there emerged what historian Owen Kelly described as 'a new kind of political activist who believed that creativity was an essential tool in any kind of radical struggle'.[29]

Montage: Have a Go and Pass it on

Although early video cameras were technically portable and relatively easy to use, they still consisted of a fairly heavy recording unit and a point-and-shoot style camera, with the option of a separate, handheld microphone for improved sound.

While this made anything more than very short recordings challenging for a single operator, it was well-suited to collaborative and shared forms of production and representation. And since video cameras were still relatively expensive and hard to come by, a single camera unit was often shared by groups of five to ten people, with each participant wanting to 'have a go' in front of and behind the camera.

This sharing of equipment allowed for the communication of diverse viewpoints and encouraged formal experimentation and collective authorship. What could broadly be considered a new 'documentary turn' began to redefine what was then the accepted mode of videography. Early videos tended to be composed of sprawling, hand-held shots, recorded in sequence and typically edited in-camera.

The spontaneous energy of the participants permeated the footage, creating a sense of urgency and intimacy; an aesthetic of activist video that has largely remained unchanged. It is a common sight in many of the videos featured in this book to show the production process. From shots of the camera and trailing microphone wires to community playback meetings and group editing sessions, activist video makers want to demystify what they do, as an invitation to the audience to get involved.

Facing page:
Top row: (clockwise from left): Inter-Action kids workshop, 1970s; *Community Video 1980* (Joel Venet, 1980); Inter-Action adults workshop, 1970s.
Middle row: left, centre: both Inter-Action kids workshop, 1970s; right: From *Basic Video in Community Work* (1975).
Bottom row: (l to r): *Starting to Happen* (Liberation Films, 1974); *Framed Youth: Revenge of the Teenage Perverts* (London Lesbian and Gay Youth Video Project, 1983).

3. HOUSING FOR ALL

Fast forward 46 years after video cameras were first used by squatters to record and resist evictions; it's 2015 on the Aylesbury housing estate in South London, and video activists Watchful Eye are carrying on this tradition. Their video, *Southwark Council Make Empty Flats on Aylesbury Estate Uninhabitable*, shows workmen, under police protection, forcefully entering and damaging squatted council housing, after Southwark Council authorised the eviction to prevent further occupation. The Aylesbury, a large housing estate built between 1963 and 1977, was once home to 7,500 residents. In January 2015, in the face of threats of demolition and redevelopment, with the displacement of many of its residents, activists began squatting one block. Their aim was to halt the demolition and document and amplify residents' demands for 'refurbishment not demolition'.[1] In response, the council boarded up the flats and made them uninhabitable. Watchful Eye began making videos on the Aylesbury as the residents struggled against planned obsolescence, gentrification and social cleansing by the council and developers. In the words of Watchful Eye: 'We watch, we listen, we support.'[2]

The video moves through the estate, the image shaking and jolting. On-screen titles explain what has already happened and what is happening now. Policemen speak over radios; residents use mobile phones. Workmen, wielding heavy machinery, cut through doors. Sparks fill the frame and sledgehammers and power tools drown out the sound of breathing from behind the camera. The video consists of wide shots of the forceful entry, intercut with travelling shots as the camera person moves through the estate to get closer to the action. The soundtrack is filled with shattering

Top: *Southwark Council make empty flats on Aylesbury Estate uninhabitable* (Watchful Eye, 2015). **Above:** *Fight for the Aylesbury* (Watchful Eye, 2017).

windows and smashed doors. Someone standing close by narrates the action as it unfolds; their face remains unseen. The camera moves between their gesturing hands and the demolition of the building they had been occupying. This same footage was later heavily edited and, with the addition of a voiceover provided by a newsreader, used by the BBC for a news

Housing Problems (Edgar Anstey / Arthur Elton, 1935).

report about the occupation and eviction. In the interest of impartiality, the report includes interviews with one resident who is angry about the occupation and grateful for the eviction and another who wishes to remain on the estate. The last word is given to a statement from Southwark Council who, without offering any evidence, claim that the majority of residents wanted to be re-housed elsewhere, rather than remain in their homes.

Housing struggles were a battleground for radical politics throughout the 20th century, and a touchstone issue for radical and progressive filmmaking. The reformist documentaries *Housing Problems* (Edgar Anstey/ Arthur Elton, 1935) and *Homes for the People* (Kay Mander, 1945) broke new ground in allowing those living in often appalling housing conditions to speak for themselves. In the 1960s and 70s, 16mm films – such as Cinema Action's *Not a Penny on The Rents* (1968) and *Squatters* (1970) – employed similar strategies to more radical effect. Video activists have gone further still, handing over the camera and allowing precariously-housed residents to document and make visible their experiences on their own terms.

Writer and activist Jan O'Malley described the situation in her neighbourhood in West London in the 1970s as a battleground between:

> profit-hungry property converters, who sold to the highest bidder, and the non-profit housing trusts, who made an attempt to allocate their housing on the basis of need. ... The scars of the battle were felt throughout the area: the eviction of present residents, spiralling house prices and luxury conversions into mews cottages and expensive town houses.[3]

At this time, the Labour Party was viewed by much of the working class as an inadequate channel through which to gain support. The Labour government's drive to rebuild inner-city neighbourhoods during the late 1960s required re-housing tenants and residents, which often meant displacing communities. Housing activism was largely organised around different grassroots strategies that aimed to destabilize confidence in the property market, forcing landlords to pull out, prices to drop and housing associations and local councils to step in.

In the decade between 1968 and 1977 over a quarter of a million people in Britain legally squatted empty houses owned by someone else, without seeking permission and without paying rent. In the North London borough of Camden, residents who were squatting or living in houses as part of 'short-life' housing schemes were put at risk of being made homeless when the council began to purchase and empty these properties for regeneration projects or demolition.

Ben's Arrest and *Squat Now While Stocks Last*, both made in 1974 by John 'Hoppy' Hopkins and fellow squatter Sue Hall (a neighbour and founder of activist group Graft On!), became exemplars for the role of video in representing and defending squatters' rights in legal proceedings.

Squat Now While Stocks Last is shot from street level, showing the ground floor of a large, crumbling semi-detached house, covered in graffiti. Out front is a police van. The frame is gradually filled by bailiffs wielding sledgehammers, flanked by police and council officers. The hammer ultimately wins out and the door, barricaded by furniture, collapses under its weight. The shaky camera pans up to the roof to try and focus on the squatters as they spray water from a hose down onto the invaders. Two

Squat Now While Stocks Last (Sue Hall / John Hopkins, 1974).

squatters try to pull a ladder up and away from a window, as others gather on the roof to escape and get a clearer view of the action, while the camera zooms in and out to take in the whole scene. After a short click and a break, the camera fizzes back into action, now nestled between the police officers, as the first of the squatters is dragged out onto the streets and into the back of the van – the camera captures scratches along his back and we hear him yell and repeat 'That's fucking democracy for you!.' From behind the camera a voice tells the viewer, 'I can see the marks on his back like you can'; the frame is then repeated and held to highlight the scratches and scuffs on his body and clothes.

After another break in the action, during which time the number of squatters on the roof has increased to five, the camera people are heard discussing the duration of the invasion: 'We've held for 35 minutes. Not bad for a Monday morning.' The action continues until each of the squatters has been roughly escorted out of the house into the van.

Although the way Hopkins and Hall's 1974 video was made and circulated differed from Watchful Eye's 2015 video, in their look and feel and the way the camera functions as a witness and a mediator between the residents and the authorities, the two videos attest to a continuity of video practice spanning generations of housing activists.

A 1974 report in the *Guardian* highlights the novelty of video as legal evidence:

> A Video Tape recording of squatters being evicted from a London home will be admissible as defence evidence in a case of alleged assault – provided that Scotland Yard forensic scientists are satisfied that the tape is authentic … Mr Peter Darcy and Dr John Pollard, who are accused of assaulting a police constable during their eviction from a house in Prince of Wales Crescent, Chalk Farm, North London, by bailiffs and police earlier this year, believe the film is crucial defence evidence … the application has been adjourned while Scotland Yard makes a duplicate and tests it thoroughly for defects and tampering … Birnberg [Defence Counsel] argued that there was no difference in principle between the recording of a human voice and a video tape.[4]

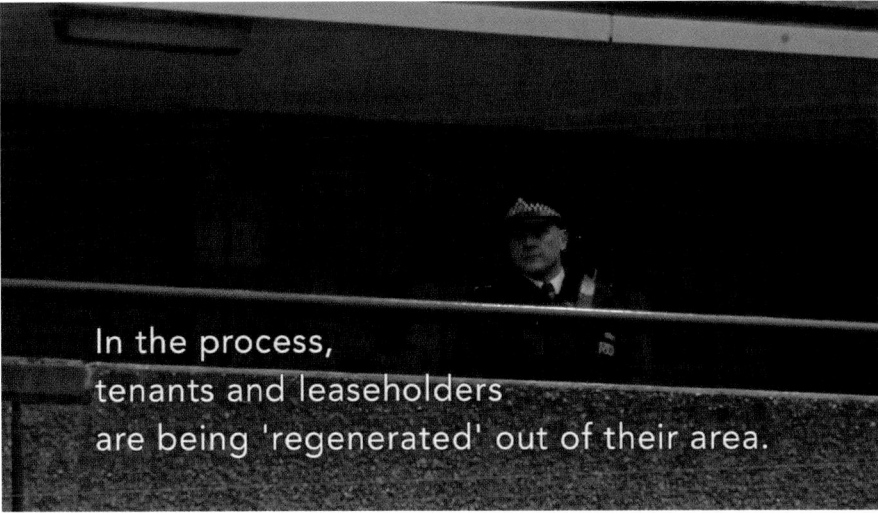

Southwark Council make empty flats on Aylesbury Estate uninhabitable (Watchful Eye, 2015).

Not surprisingly, the police viewed this legal precedent with trepidation, as well they might: the Defence's use of video proved successful, and the suspects were acquitted. Not only did the video prove to be valuable evidence in court, but the suspects' ability to study the recording of the eviction together was crucial in clarifying the sequence of events and undermining the Prosecution's case:

> when the police came to give their evidence it was so transparently, obviously faked ... as a piece of social action, getting 15 or 20 people off of police charges ... it was a beneficial act, which couldn't have been done without video.[5]

The aesthetic of videos documenting evictions has remained largely unchanged since the 1970s: the handheld camera, following the action as it unfolds in real time, sways and zooms today just as it did then. Both videos show policemen, council officials and bailiffs using heavy machinery to break down the front doors of the squatted buildings. In lieu of subtitles, the 1974 video lingers on white graffiti on the outside of the building, spelling out the occupiers' demands: 'HOUSES FOR ALL'. Soundtracks of both videos contrast hushed commands between the officials and chants and jeers from the residents. In the case of *Squat Now While Stocks Last*, once the eviction has taken place, and the squatters have been dragged from the building by the police, the voice from behind the camera is recorded making observations and unanswered requests to the authorities for information.

Both videos appeared in BBC reports, but following the broadcast of the 1974 video, Sue Hall was given equal time to contextualise the action shown on screen.[6] An article in *Time Out* described that broadcast as 'one of the most memorable pieces of television this year', drawing attention to the specific aesthetics of the footage, with its look and feel of intimacy and liveness. While this has since become commonplace on news broadcasts, it clearly felt strikingly raw and unfamiliar at the time:

> The swaying and confusion of the handheld camera mirrored the chaos and anxiety at the scene. When a cop threatened the cameraman, he seemed to be threatening the viewer as well.[7]

The activism in both these videos, made over 40 years apart, is located in the act of bearing witness, producing evidence of and a counternarrative to the violent actions of the police and local authorities. These 'witness videos' continue to make up the bulk of video activism. Examples include the work of Watchful Eye as well as other housing activist groups such as Living Rent in Scotland. These groups make videos of acts of injustice and abuse carried out by local councils and landlords, and document their demonstrations against these injustices. When footage of these actions is shared on social media it often shames and embarrasses the perpetrators into responding.

While witness videos tend to be made and shared with urgency, video has also been taken up by housing activists to support and represent precariously housed residents in more involved and sustained ways. Sue Hall was living in short-life housing in North London when, in 1972, she began carrying out experiments using video in the service of squatters and other residents like herself living in insecure housing. Together they formed the activist group Graft On!, with the urgent objective to resist the demolition and redevelopment of their neighbourhood. The group took its name from the area its members lived in – Grafton Terrace, not far from the Institute for Research and Technology. In a document co-written by Hall and her collaborator John 'Hoppy' Hopkins, they describe the work of Graft On! as 'communications research', integrating video with ongoing grassroots activism: 'An action research agency applying communication theory to social change.'[8] Hall compared their use of video to the ethnographic research method known as 'participant observation' to explain how, through the shared production of videos, they were able to engage with residents on local issues, to whose experiences they directly related:

> We were squatters ourselves, we were not from the outside. And at first people were very hesitant about the video, and we took it out and let other people handle it a lot. We showed them, this is what you do, this is how you zoom, this is how you focus ... But after people had had a go themselves, they felt reassured. They didn't see it as dangerous, or outside, or any of those things. And that was quite crucial. And we videoed occupations, parties, evictions, street actions, lectures, seminars and marches.[9]

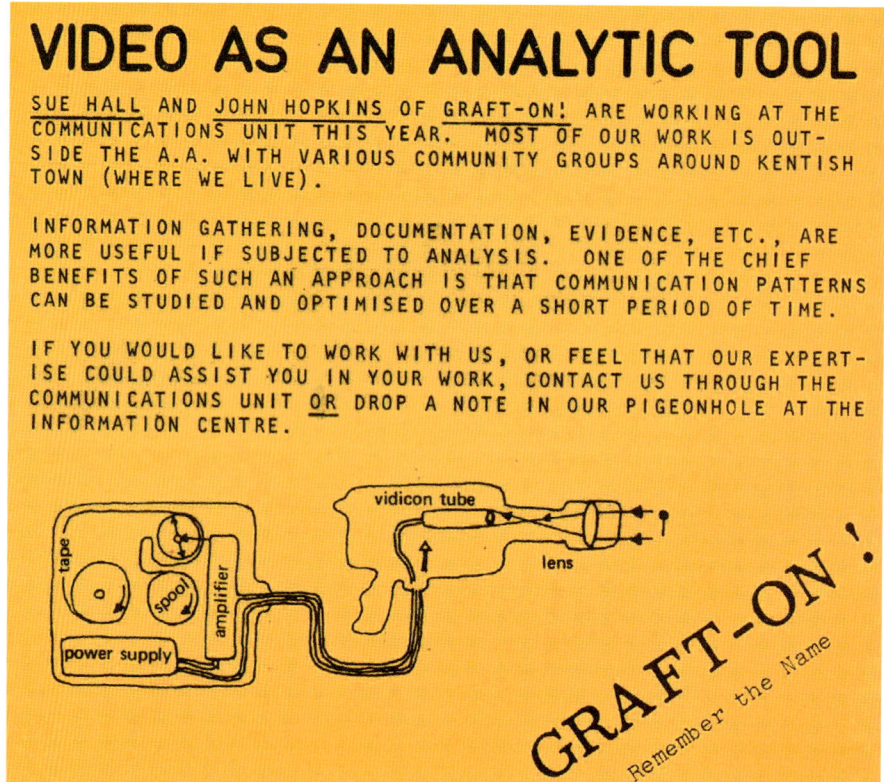

Promotion for Graft On! (1974).

Graft On! were influenced by the socially-engaged approaches developed by Montreal's Challenge for Change, which Hopkins had observed during his research trip to Canada. Aware of the risk of 'parachuting' themselves into communities outside of their own, Hall distanced their work from that of Challenge for Change, which operated on a top-down model initiated and funded by the state: 'the only communities we ever worked with were ones we belonged to ourselves … we didn't believe in telling other people what was best for them.'[10]

Since his first video efforts in 1969, Hopkins had been experimenting with how to produce activist video projects to improve communication between those in precarious housing situations and those with the power to effect change. 'At the time,' he admitted, 'this was possibly pushing the technology beyond its limits, attempting to achieve quality suitable for public service use.' In 1971 he made a documentary, *Livin' Free*, about the beginnings of the squatting community he lived in.[11] Although shot on 16mm film (access to video editing was beyond his means), it was subsequently transferred to 1/2-inch black-and-white video to facilitate easy playback and distribution. Hopkins would go on to exploit the ease of use and distribution of video alongside the superior editing facility that film allowed, producing a series of housing videos that attempted not only to document housing struggles, but to change them.

In 1972, as an experiment in bridging the communication gap between the council and residents, Hopkins co-produced *Camden Housing Film for Camden Council* with the radical video group TVX.[12] It featured the council's director of housing giving advice about housing law and rent rebates. Once again, the work was both shot and edited on film, and then transferred to video for screening. An article in *Time Out* explains that this production enabled the deputy chairman of housing for Camden, who was too afraid to meet the local squatters for fear of 'being verbally maligned', to watch and respond to pre-recorded discussions of residents talking about their difficulties with short-life housing policy.[13] Following the production of these video projects *about* housing issues, Hall and Hopkins embarked on an activist video project that would be *for* and *from* their community of squatters.

During the late 1960s, as part of the Labour government's plans to redevelop inner city areas, tenants and residents were often invited to futile 'community consultations' only to find themselves evicted and re-housed outside of their neighbourhoods shortly afterwards.[14] As a concession to the precariously-housed residents living around Grafton Terrace and Prince of Wales Crescent, between 1973 and 1974 Camden Council organised a public consultation, labelled 'Participation in Planning', which saw circulars distributed and notices placed in local newspapers inviting the public to meet and contribute to the future planning of their neighbourhood. For Sue Hall, it was the moment that video and activism combined:

> I was working very hard to get local allies to support us and also to get interest from the squatters, who weren't exactly easy to convince that they

should indulge in these strange bureaucratic practices … So while I was doing this Hoppy approached me and he said "What about making a video?"[15]

As a first step towards engaging other residents to use video as part of their activism, Hall took a video camera to a meeting about the proposed 'road network and environmental area scheme'. According to Hall, the proposal

was a conspiracy to put main roads near estates in working class areas and to fence off and ban traffic in upper middle class enclaves … it was social engineering, trying to creep under the radar in the guise of "participation".[16]

Videotapes of the meeting's results were shared with interested parties, including other groups of squatters and trade unions. Graft On! also screened the recordings at further meetings with councillors. After one such presentation, Hall recalls council members shouting angrily at one another as they witnessed their colleagues describing the new planning propositions. However, when the council's original proposals went ahead largely unchanged, Hall realised that the odds were stacked against the residents: 'the policy didn't take any notice of what we were doing … we had to follow them, not them us.'[17]

Changing tactics, the group established the first residents' association of squatters and those in short-life housing, and produced a video explaining how others in similar conditions might do the same. The 14-minute *Forming a Residents Association*, made in 1974, documents a meeting held with 35 precariously-housed residents living in in the same North London neighbourhood. The residents are shown attempting to formalise their loose group into a more formal organisation in a bid to win recognition from the council and a say in how they are housed and treated. A voiceover describes the video as 'the crystallisation of their attempts to participate in the planning process,' and outlines the different stages of their plan to engage the wider community.

The video shows the period of 'pre-publicity' ahead of the meeting: talking with other interested parties to get their support and input, publicly displaying alternative plans, printing and distributing of handbills and fly posters, issuing a press release and, on the day of the meeting, putting up additional posters and signage in local streets. The remainder of the video takes place at the meeting, which begins with a presentation of the alternative plans for the neighbourhood drawn up by some members of the group. These are displayed with transparent overlays so that attendees can write or draw their suggestions over them. An agenda is shown pasted up on a wall. Previous video recordings are also played to help explain what has happened so far. The meeting is chaired by Hopkins, who tells the group that 'it doesn't work to behave like a group of talented individuals' ... the best way to get something done if you have to interface with the public is by forming a residents' association, because this is what *they* recognise'. A discussion follows, with residents taking turns to speak and input their ideas. It's clear that the videomakers have no ulterior motive other than to use the meeting and, by extension, the video to share information and strategies, to hear different opinions and make a space for disagreements, and to recognise and record these.

The recording functions as a minute-taker. At one point a vote is taken; at another, a list of people who have agreed to help with the organisation of the group is read out. One group member suggests that too many meet-

Forming a Residents Association (Graft On!, 1974).

ings can cause 'burn-out' and that instead they should alternate between meetings and actions. At times we are reminded of the novelty of the video camera: at one point, as it pans around the room, one participant, who up until this moment has been rather sober and practical, breaks into a smile, waves at the camera and exclaims 'Hello Mum!' The video ends with a set of hand-written credits, aptly accompanied by The Rolling Stones' 'You Can't Always Get What You Want'. The credits are interrupted by a shot of Sue Hall holding a microphone and adopting the pose of a news reporter. Mimicking the rhetoric of broadcast television, she directly addresses the audience:

> So far, so good. Of course this activity has no meaning unless something really changes. Will the residents' plans ever see the light of day? Will the Council accept them? This story has already been running for some years. So watch out for the next exciting episode!

The camera gave the residents access to a broader audience, and the production of the video galvanised them into action. Graft On! prioritised serving local residents in short-life housing and the squatting community, a sector of society they identified as suffering from social rejection and a deficit of democratic rights. The producers counted themselves among the subjects seeking representation, which spurred them on to develop methods in an urgent and responsive way, sensitive to the needs of the group. Because members of the community were positioned both in front of and behind the camera, their own experiences motivated the methodology, which unfolded and evolved according to their needs and in a language appropriate to their experiences.

The work of Graft On! and the production of *Forming a Residents' Association* provide an early example of the shift from the production of 'action tapes' to the production of 'process tapes'. Action tapes involve the use of video in 'situations where people were taking action on an issue';[18] documenting and bearing witness to struggles. The joint production of action tapes provided an opportunity for residents to raise issues about life in a particular housing estate or neighbourhood. By contrast, process tapes use the act of making a video to move the action forward while simultaneously mediating and providing a record of the flow of events. In the case

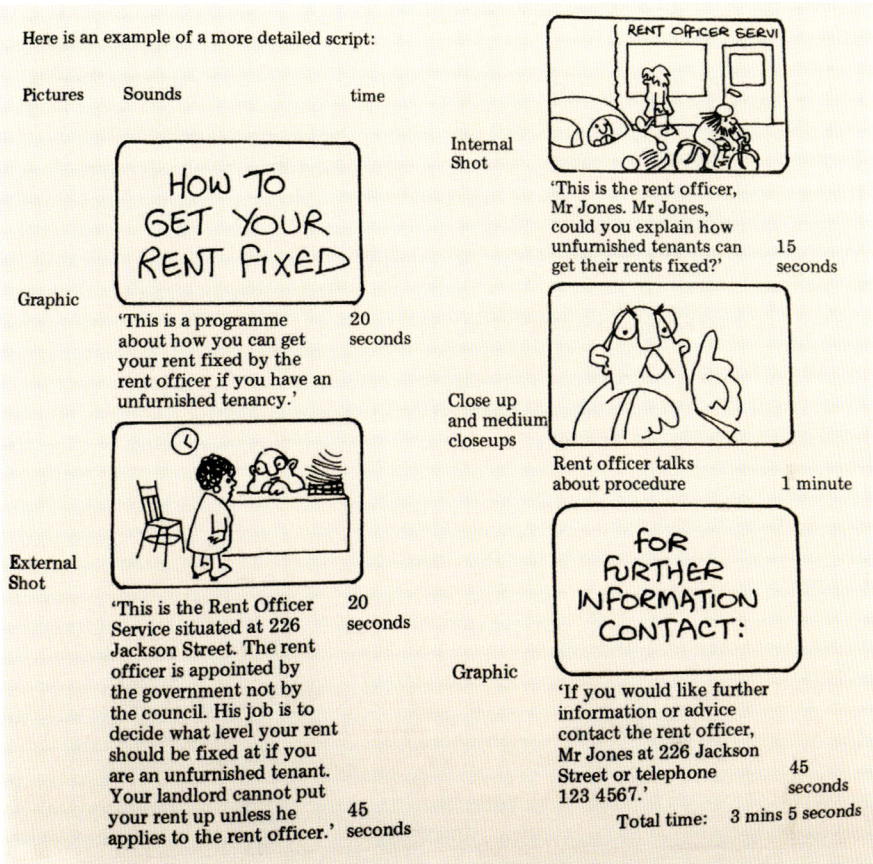

Example script, from *Basic Video in Community Work* (1975).

of *Forming a Residents' Association*, the finished process tape traces each step the group went through in establishing and organising their group. It was the intention that the finished video would serve as an 'instructional/educational tape ... hired by local groups in other parts of the country'[19], so that residents with similar housing needs could restage the steps carried out in the video.

Meanwhile, action tapes continued to proliferate during the 1970s and 80s. One particularly common variety came to be known as 'damp tapes'. These projects documented poor housing conditions: not only problems with damp, but also black mould, leaky ceilings, unsafe walkways, overflowing bins, broken windows and inadequate provisions or services. The compilations would then be played back on a monitor at tenants' meetings or during appointments with a council officer. Whereas issues presented as distinct, one-off complaints could be easily ignored, combining multiple and diverse issues gave the videos an impact that was harder to overlook.

The Albany Video 'damp tapes' project was started in 1974, when John White, a community worker based at The Albany Art Centre in South London, began working with members of the newly-formed residents association on the nearby Pepys Estate in Deptford. The project documented the poor upkeep of the estate, and the lack of social and community facilities, such as childcare and support for isolated parents. This material was shown together at a community association public meeting attended by representatives of the Greater London Council (GLC). Here White explains his relationship to the residents, his aims and the specific role of video:

> Quite quickly I got into doing something that the tenants association wanted me to do because there was always repairs and maintenance work that wasn't getting done and the authority, the GLC, was quite distant and so they were always campaigning and complaining about estate maintenance and repairs and improvements. And what you could do with the video camera was document stuff so they could see a use for that. And I put together several different mini documentaries showing the state of the estate and what needed repairing.[20]

Action tapes produced to support housing campaigns were concerned as much with using video to raise awareness about specific housing struggles as they were with the groups impacted by the struggles coming together and taking authorship of the content. Andy Porter, who was making similar action tapes with residents in West London, reflected on the strengths of one such project:

> It was put together by local people. It had given them the power not to just shout and rave at the authorities about how bad conditions were. It allowed them to express themselves, to actually bring their living conditions right into the very room where they were meeting the councillors, where they were totally undeniable.[21]

A number of video projects expanded the idea of the damp tape to facilitate longer-term process-tape projects, including *Don't Talk Wet – Dry Up* (1983), produced in Newcastle by Swingbridge Media with the North Kenton Residents Group, and *Dampbusters* (1990), a video of a play produced by Easthall Residents' Association in Glasgow.

Increasing access to ever-more portable video recording technology – and, later, to the diverse, wide-reaching distribution platforms made possible by smartphones, the Internet and social media – has seen housing activist groups in the UK continue to use video in comparable ways to earlier video activists. In 2020, during the Covid-19 pandemic, the activist group Housing Action Southwark and Lambeth[22] invited its members living in overcrowded and temporary accommodation to use their smartphones

Pepys Estate – Organising (Albany Video, 1974).

to record the impact on their families of ongoing government-sanctioned Covid quarantine measures combined with overcrowded, inadequate housing provision.

The videos, recorded from the point of view of the residents, take the form of short tours of cramped housing, with families of four or five people often sharing just one or two rooms. To illustrate the widespread impact and scale of the problems being faced by the residents, the short video tours are edited together back-to-back, as was the case with the damp tapes. The compilations were shared on Twitter rather than distributed through public events and meetings, and the housing developers and council officials implicated in the action were tagged, named and shamed instead of being invited to screening events. The videos also look similar to those made in the 1970s, with minimal editing and action narrated from behind the handheld camera. The viewer is invited into the home of the videomaker, and not addressed as an outsider, creating a feeling of intimacy.

By the 1980s the realist aesthetic of action tapes and process videos was expanded upon by activist groups looking to produce more complex videos in the service of ongoing housing struggles experienced by minority groups. In 1984 Carol Stevens and Karen Alexander from Albany Video collaborated with young women's theatre group Second Wave to make a video project called *A Netful of Holes*, based on Second Wave's stage production of the same name about the lived experience of the housing crisis and its effect on the group. Part of a wider movement of community and political theatre groups, Second Wave was based in the same building as Albany Video, and devised plays with local young women about their experiences. In the words of some of its writers, '*A Netful of Holes* is a play without a main story, rather it is a series of impressions, descriptions and scenes created around the themes of home and leaving home.'[23] The final play was the result of 11 months of workshops, discussions and research carried out by the performers into the causes and effects of homelessness among women. It was performed at the Albany Empire Theatre in November 1984.[24] Once again, an emphasis was placed on collaboration, process and establishing forms of representation specific to the experiences of the participants, while the video of the play aimed to spark discussion and further engagement:

Lockdown Diaries (Housing Action Southwark & Lambeth, 2020).

> The style of the devised work is loose, authentic and belongs to no single writer … these extracts should be used to trigger ideas, develop the work further and to simulate discussion.'[25]

What was new, and fed into developments in activist videos, was the combination of real-life experiences with speculative and performance elements, in which different scenarios and outcomes could be tried out safely and carefully. Theatre groups like Second Wave encouraged the participants to choose what they wanted to show and control how they expressed themselves: 'You are doing rather than watching; you are making things happen all around you.'[26]

Unlike the stage play, the tape is able to intercut scenes of the final performance with process footage including group discussions and improv-

Hostile Housing (London Renters Union, 2019).

isation workshops. This structure gives an impression of the working process leading up to the finished play and enabled further discussion at screening events. The extra scenes set out the different stages that went into producing the play, including snapshots of tours of hostels and rehearsals, as well as participants discussing their experiences of living at home, leaving home and the problems of finding somewhere to live. The introduction to the video explains that none of the women involved had any previous drama experience, and goes on to show how the workshops were designed to build up their confidence and 'raise their consciousness about certain things, and about themselves.'[27]

The experimentation with the realist mode in action and process videos introduced the potential to add layers of complexity to the processes employed in earlier activist videos, providing a space for reflection and for exploring new perspectives. Combining participants' lived experiences with character work, poetry and roleplay invited more open-ended and potentially less extractive or harmful engagement than did previous approaches to activist video production. Instead, those involved were invited to imagine and bring to life alternative outcomes to those they were currently facing. The cultural theorist Kobena Mercer has described this shift away from a homogenous, 'monologic tendency' towards a 'dialogic tendency', which is able to 'overcome reality' and respond to the 'diverse and complex qualities'[28] of the varied lived experiences of the subjects – who, in the case of activist videos, are also the producers.

The collaboration between Albany Video and Second Wave is indicative of the new reflective and expanded approach being developed by video groups in the 1980s. This approach has continued to be used and developed by contemporary housing activist groups, as evidenced by a 2019 video project called *Our Homes*, initiated by the London Renters Union (LRU).[29] The community of union members involved in the project used terminology and methods developed by Graft On!, described as 'Participatory Action Research'. Everyone who took part received support and training from video pioneers Jackie Shaw and Clive Robertson, who had founded the participatory video and creative storytelling organisation 'Real Time' in 1984 and co-authored the first definitive guide to participatory video in 1997.[30] The project produced a video series, *Hostile Housing* (2020), which explored themes including homelessness, single motherhood, the impact of migration, racism and the failures of the criminal justice system.

As with *A Netful of Holes*, participants brought their own experiences and stories to share, while the videos comprise material recorded and gathered by those involved, including group discussions and interviews intercut with poetic and dramatised scenes. For those involved in the LRU project, making the video functioned as an extension of their organising and activism. The intentions of the video project were aligned with the values of LRU, including a focus on taking action and building power, while those involved aimed to increase knowledge and understanding of the issues facing renters and intended the finished video to be used as a tool for political action, further organising and building solidarity with local community groups. The production process included oral history and camera training as well as a series of iterative discussions about the shape and direction the video might take. The group did not identify as video activists, but rather as activists and organisers using video to learn from one another and develop tools to support their work and share their experiences; what connected them was the way in which the housing crisis left them disempowered and isolated.

The impact of austerity measures and funding cuts was felt by the members involved during the process of making the video, and features in discussions throughout. In one group discussion, a member, clearly exhausted by the housing system and feeling safe in the group and on camera, takes the opportunity to critique the structures that control her living situation: 'Who,' she asks, 'benefits from this?' Poignantly, the question goes unanswered. In another scene, a member creates a performance on a busy street, mapping out a floorplan in lines of tape stuck to the pavement of the cramped single room she shared with her two children in a hostel. It was important for those making the video that it didn't function merely as a 'nice bit of outreach', but would also provide a space for them to share their myriad experiences in a form of collective representation. A lack of access to funding and public spaces to host meetings proved challenging, costly and time-consuming, while the stress and constraints placed on the members due to their housing issues also meant that contributors sometimes struggled to find the time and energy to commit to the project. The minimal funding the group managed to raise was used to cover the hire of space for meetings and equipment, and to pay for the time of eight members to take part. Such limitations circumscribed what the project was able to achieve – and provide a counter to the rhetoric that increased access to technology and distribution networks necessarily empower and make video activism 'easier'.

Nevertheless, video continues to provide a means to galvanise people living in precarious housing conditions to build solidarity and take action, in a housing environment grown increasingly hostile since the end of the 1970s. The Conservative government's 'Right to Buy' policy, introduced in 1980, gave local authority tenants the opportunity to buy their homes at a reduced rate but returned only a fraction of the proceeds to the councils themselves. The result was a rapid depletion of the supply of genuinely affordable social housing, with many tenants in private rented accommodation or temporary housing made homeless. With the sweeping away of rent controls and other regulations governing landlords (another Thatcher-era policy), the historic 'safety nets' for homeless people have largely been removed. Meanwhile, waves of gentrification have forced up rent and house prices, exposing many social and council tenants to the threat of being 'decanted': rehoused out of their communities and far from their support networks to make way for affluent young professionals or for private investors looking to park their money.

At a grassroots and local level, the production and distribution of housing activist videos persists as an attainable means for those affected to relate their experiences and relay them to the relevant authorities, that is, those who perpetuate them and have the power to resolve them. For residents living in substandard homes or under threat of eviction, the modern equivalents of action tapes still function as evidence to build cases and attest to their experiences. With easy access to video recording technology and the means to self-distribute using social media channels, residents are able to communicate between themselves, as well as with local authorities, and collectively represent their shared experiences. For isolated residents, involvement in the production of a more sustained process video can provide a means to build intersectional solidarity and connect with the communities and neighbourhoods in which they live. Once housing activism combines with video activism, housing issues are no longer the problem of individual households; they are socialised and shared, increasing the prospect of effecting meaningful change. From these beginnings, it is possible to build a movement that understands housing as a human right and demands 'Housing for All!'.

Close-up: From Newsreel to *Reel News*

For as long as there have been mainstream news media, there have been attempts to provide alternatives to them. As early as 1929, when the newsreel was king, the Federation of Workers Film Societies was formed to:

> encourage the formation of local workers' film societies... make arrangements for the supply of films or apparatus required by such societies... To advise local workers film societies on the best methods of carrying on their work... [and] to encourage the production of films of value to the working-class.[31]

The Federation focused initially on licensing and distributing suitable films and on creating a network of film societies around the UK. But in 1931, it launched its own production fund to support the creation of films about the lives of workers. The fund's aims were strikingly reminiscent of those of the video activists decades later:

> We have to found film agitprop troops, i.e. small collectives, which are in very close touch with the factories and agricultural workers. Their members must be 'worker film correspondents' who not only record demonstrations and other big campaigns of the workers, but also make regular film reports from the factories and the countryside.[32]

As well as agitating around the rights and fair representation of workers, the Federation supported films about imperialist struggles further afield and the rising

Reel News: Orgreave Truth & Justice Campaign (2019).

tide of fascism closer to home. In 1933 the Workers' Theatre Movement established a film section, Kino, to oversee the distribution of agitprop films from Soviet Russia. A year later a production arm was set up to produce the *Workers Newsreel*, 'to present NEWS from the working-class point of view.'

Well into the 21st century, video activists are employing similarly networked approaches to production in pursuit of comparable goals, as we find in the stated aims of the contemporary collective *Reel News*:

> Reel News uses film as an active tool in creating change, grounded in our belief in social and economic justice and the centrality of the working class in achieving change. We aim to amplify the voices of struggles on the ground to help campaigns achieve victories, make information available and facilitate communication between different struggles.[33]

Formed in 2006 out of the Indymedia movement of the 1990s, *Reel News* responded to mainstream media's sidelining and misrepresentation of the struggles of ordinary people by applying 'be your own media' principles to supporting progressive working-class movements, particularly in the workplace. Its bi-monthly newsreel promotes workers' rights and industrial action, campaigns against police surveillance and trade union blacklisting, and draws attention to the Climate Emergency in the UK and overseas. Its videos are shared through its YouTube channel and Facebook page, as well as at regular in-person events.

While harkening back to the revolutionary use of film in Soviet Russia, *Reel News* is named in homage to the American 'alternative newsreel' movement, whose members took up 16mm cameras to shape a counternarrative to mainstream news in the 1960s, supporting the work of the Black Panthers and documenting protests against the Vietnam War. These films were distributed in the UK in the 1970s by *Liberation Films* and inspired their members to make their own films.

Based in London, *Reel News* is led by founder and sole full-time member Shaun Dey, previously a trade union shop steward. The wider collective comprises activists and skilled individuals from different media fields who contribute based on the group's activities and the campaigns they are involved in at any time. Currently the longest-running radical newsreel in British film history,[34] *Reel News* is driven by the same imperatives that drove the alternative newsreels of the 1930s: 'In the global war between rich and poor, we need news from the frontline'.

4. STARTING TO HAPPEN

By 1975, a formula had been established: 'GROUP OF PEOPLE + VIDEO' = the starting point for sharing issues, building movements and influencing authorities. This formula was expressed in a diagram in 'Basic Video in Community Work', a 1975 pamphlet published by the community arts group Inter-Action, and marked an attempt to illustrate the ways portable video cameras were being used to activate and engage groups and individuals in the production of early activist videos in the UK. The same year, Middlesex Polytechnic published a report, 'Theories and Practices of Video Work', expanding on the uses of video technology. The report identified two distinct purposes for video recorders, each pointing to early definitions of activist video: as 'media reform' to critique and counter mainstream, broadcast television, and as an 'organising tool' to bring community groups together. In line with the development of video activism, in many of the projects cited in the report, video was used to achieve 'educational, social or political objectives.'[1]

At this time, video was largely understood by activists either as an organising tool for 'communication activity of a self-generating sort within the community', or as a 'communication activity originated by an outsider, for the purposes of an existing community'.[2] In broad terms, we can think of the former as the 'insider' approach and the latter as the 'outsider' approach. These terms should not necessarily be understood as discrete positions, but rather as modes of use carried out on a spectrum, with a third, more fluid 'hybrid' approach, in between. Both diagram and report serve to highlight the significant role that process has played in the development and understanding of video activism.[3]

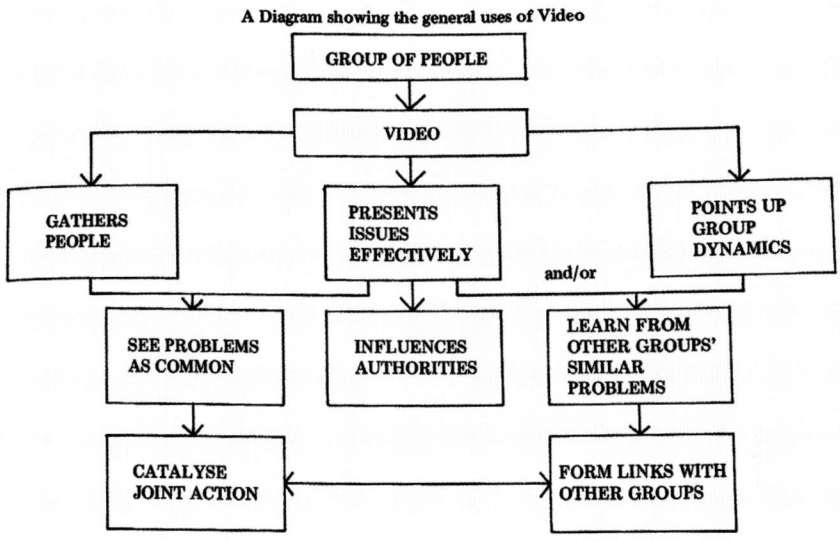

General uses of video, from *Basic Video in Community Work* (1975).

'Insider' activist video groups tend to be based in a single geographic area, with a focus on setting up long-term video resources to benefit local residents. These might include squatters, tenants associations, childcare groups or co-operatives.[4] These groups arise out of resistance to local social and political conditions – such as housing struggles, cuts to education or violent policing – which negatively affect the neighbourhoods where members of the video groups live and work. First-hand experiences shape the specific use of video for the benefit of the communities involved. As access to video recording technology proliferated and the focus of social and political movements shifted, insider activist video groups also formed along lines of identity and experience, such as race, gender and sexuality. The originators of insider video projects are also their protagonists, developing production processes intuitively. The instincts and experiences of the participants dictate what is shown and expressed, and the finished videos are characterised by urgency and a sense of intimacy.

'Outsider' activist video groups tend to use video as an organising tool to work peripatetically with different communities, neighbourhoods and identity groups. Creative frameworks, tailored towards the specific context

Community Video 1980 (Joel Venet / Liberation Films, 1980).

they are working in, centre the needs and experiences of the participants they are collaborating with at the time. The processes adopted by outsider activist video projects are also sensitive and responsive to the social context in which a project is being developed. They do, however, tend to share a number of identifiable similarities, including an iterative structure, a mediator based in the community or neighbourhood in which the project takes place, a structured plan for introducing video recording technology to the group and opportunities for participants to watch, discuss and reflect on the recorded material at regular intervals.

By drawing attention to and politicising the production and distribution of activist video projects, outsider facilitators – who might not directly identify with the experiences of the participants they are working with – contribute to the agency of participants and reduce concerns about 'parachuting in' and instrumentalising the voices and experiences of others. The aim of many outsider activist video projects is for the roles of the participants and the facilitators to begin to swap and merge, at which point the production processes begin to take on a hybrid form of both insider and outsider approaches.

The methods developed by Liberation Films, an activist film and video group established in North London in 1972, provide a useful example of the processes that an 'outsider' group implement when working with a community group they don't identify as being part of. Liberation Films emerged from the Angry Arts Film Society, which organised discussion screenings and distributed political films, a process that opened its members' eyes to the political potential of showing and ultimately making their own political films and videos. The political screenings arranged by Angry Arts had three aims that collectively determined how and why they would go on to initiate video projects: first, to draw together a wide cross-section of people; second, to identify shared areas of concern; and third, to work collectively towards affecting social change at a local level. To foster dialogue and active participation among audience members, the screenings they organised emulated the American Newsreel 'discussion-screening' format, in which 'the structure of the screening had as much priority as the structure of the film.'[5] Aligning

Liberation Films workplace playback.

the viewing context with a political responsibility was a distinctive feature of Newsreel's work: the film theorist and historian Bill Nichols notes that this 'placed into sharper relief, for other activists to see, the question of audience and of the viewing event itself as a vital part of the politics of filmmaking.'[6] As Angry Arts and Liberation Films member Sue Crockford remembers,

> We wanted to share the awakening these films had given us ... These films were so real, so unlike anything on the BBC news – above all with a point of view which thought it was important to ask questions about why a strike or demonstration was happening in the first place – that we weren't surprised people wanted to see them ... A strong part of our philosophy was wanting films to be a spark or trigger for interaction between people.[7]

The founding members of Angry Arts and Liberation Films met through their shared involvement in the Vietnam Solidarity Campaign (VSC), which went on to inform their production methods. Alongside Sue Crockford, who produced political plays and posters with the VSC, other members also active in the VSC were Tony Wickert, a disillusioned director working at the BBC, and husband and wife Geoff and Marie Richman, who wrote articles for the VSC newsletter, staged political theatre events in parks and on street corners in an attempt to engage with people outside of their intellectual ghetto, and contributed to the production of *End of a Tactic* (1969), a 16mm documentary about the Left's ambivalent relationship to protests and marches. Inspired by the burgeoning women's movement, Crockford subsequently became involved – along with Wickert – in the production of *A Woman's Place*, a 30-minute, 16mm documentary filmed at the 1970 Oxford Women's Liberation conference and the 1971 Women's Liberation March.

Around the same time, activist groups in London were beginning to gain access to portable video, and it wasn't long before Liberation Films formed to collectively organise, produce and distribute their own activist video projects that related to grassroots struggles and the specific experiences of their audiences. Liberation Films first started using video as part of their post-screening discussions, enabling audience members to record their thoughts and feedback on what they had been watching. The video tapes could then be replayed to new audiences, sparking new connections and

A Woman's Place (Liberation Films, 1971).

sometimes community-led video projects. One such playback session, at an event in Hackney, East London, led to the formation of a group which went on to establish a new playground for local children.

The first Liberation Films project to place the use of video at its centre followed in 1973, and combined the production of video material made by, for and about the residents of a specific community with repeated playback of this material for feedback and reflection. The impetus for this was, explained Geoff Richman, 'a real need for a good film about community life in Britain that community groups could use to stimulate thought and action.'[8] The aptly-named *Project Octopus* was an eight-stage video process, carried out with a community action group based in Balham, South London. It resulted in the production of a series of short videos about different issues affecting the residents involved in the project, and a 40-minute documentary, *Starting to Happen* (1974), which combined observational footage of the project, shot

Liberation Films community film show.

by members of Liberation Films on 16mm film, with video recorded by the participants. The two different media, and the way they are used, illustrate the dichotomy at the heart of the project. Where the 'outsider' Liberation Films crew used film both to document the process and to offer instruction, signifying distance and authority, the 'insider' community groups used video to carry out interviews with one another and to document relevant events in their daily lives. In contrast to the filmed elements, the grainy video material appears closer to the action and evokes a feeling of authenticity and informality. Project Octopus, and the documentary it produced, adopted a linear, instructional structure to present the stages a community might go through when using video cameras as an organising tool to shoot, edit and screen a video to highlight local issues and effect change.[9]

A breakdown of these stages serves to illustrate the ways video was – and may still be – used as an organising tool by an outsider activist group. Stage one involved making contact with a community group who were enthusiastic about participating in a video project. The need to be invited into a community and to focus on the facilitation of possible ideas, rather than directing the project itself, continued to be a guiding principal for outsider activist video practitioners. *Video in Community Development*, a practical handbook on the use of video by grassroots groups published in 1972, included a section titled 'Project Requirements',[10] which proposed that, when setting up a video project with and for a community, the groups should prioritise communication processes from within the community, and not the needs of outside researchers. The handbook goes on to stress the need for flexibility and to argue that the determination of a project's form should be dictated by the community.[11]

Stage two saw members of Liberation Films, following their careful introduction to the neighbourhood, return to shoot a short 16mm 'trigger film' about the area, interviewing local residents about their attitudes to living in Balham and their feelings about local community activities and services. The completed trigger film was then shown at a 'Community Film Show' as the finale of a programme of films about community-led activities. To make these film shows accessible to as many people as possible, they were often

Starting to Happen (Liberation Films, 1974).

Starting to Happen (Liberation Films, 1972).

held in a local hall, library or social space and publicised widely with posters, flyers and advertisements. After each screening, group discussions were facilitated by members of Liberation Films, providing an opportunity for the audience to talk about themselves and the place where they lived, with the trigger film providing a shared focal point to reflect on.

Stage three, which followed right after this discussion, saw the team encourage audience members to use video cameras to interview one other and identify possible subjects for a video project. These videos were then played back to the group so they could appreciate the way video could be used to support discussions. The group would then collectively decide which subjects they would like to explore further: in the case of Project Octopus, the themes selected included the mismanagement of litter and waste, the lack of youth services and unsafe road crossing for children. The audience was then divided into groups, who were invited to take part in training to make their own video tapes investigating the issues they had identified.

For stage four, facilitators were urged to exercise caution when it came to overseeing participants' first experiences with video recording equipment:

1. Consider very carefully the first moves you make with video. At its introduction it has the added strength of fascination, and careless use at this point could easily destroy what confidence has been built up already
2. Arrange properly publicised playback sessions from time to time open to the whole community
3. Prepare to train members of the community in the use of video should anyone be interested [12]

In Project Octopus, audience members were introduced to the portable video recording equipment through a series of games and exercises, with an emphasis on fun and experimentation rather than technical skills. Attendees were trained in the basic use of the cameras through, for example, recording *vox pop* interviews in the neighbourhood, which were used to gather ideas and explore what issues might be important to other members of the community. Once the objectives of the group were discussed and agreed, members of Liberation Films began to step back, playing the part of facilitators, providing support and guidance while finding ways for the group to lead.

Stage five saw the group come together several times to view and assess the video material they had recorded. Together with the Liberation Films team, they decided how to edit and structure the final video, and agreed on a date and format for presenting the finished video to the community. *Video in Community Development* further emphasised the role of playback by proposing that facilitators should make it possible for the participants to view all of the footage that had been recorded, as soon as possible after it had been shot and ideally before editing. This meant that participants could choose to erase any parts they considered unsuitable for the public, while the facilitator would be able to 'show adequately how the uses of the video tape will, or can be, beneficial to themselves and other people like themselves.'[13]

Stage six involved organising a screening event, similar to the first community film show, which was advertised throughout the neighbourhood with posters and flyers inviting the community to watch the completed video and be part of a discussion. TV monitors were used for small group discussions and equal emphasis was given to entertainment and lively debate.

Starting to Happen (Liberation Films, 1972).

Stage seven featured the creation of a compilation bringing together the film material recorded by Liberation Films and the video shot by participants.

Stage eight saw the community group encouraged to use what they had made as a new trigger film and to take the compilation film to other communities and set up community film shows there. This final stage reflects the objectives of many activist video projects: for new groups to form and make and share their own videos – without the support of the outsider video group.

An effective activist video project typically requires an element of interchange and hybridity between the roles of insider and outsider. Su Braden, reflecting on a decade of experience working as an artist in communities in her 1980 book *Artists and People*, asserts that the practitioner working with a community group should ideally spend enough time within that community to establish 'fluidity'[14] and pave the way for a reciprocal exchange.[15] The facilitator should be introduced by a mediator or interlocutor located within the community they wish to work with. Together they can then be responsible for the 'formulation of the idea ... and management of the scheme.'[16] Proposals, Braden stresses, 'should include ways of independently evaluating each scheme, and this implies that there should be some definition of objectives from the outset.'[17]

The production processes and content of activist videos rely on discussion and collaboration, with the needs of participants informing the focus of each. The techniques specific to early video activism allowed participants to reject the passivity that media invariably imposes on its subjects, and instead assert their control over their representation on screen. For many early activist video projects, the ultimate goal was for participants to become fluent and confident enough with the means of production to become community videomakers themselves.

One exponent of this third, hybrid approach is the work of Manchester Film and Video Workshop (formerly Manchester Independent Filmmakers Association), established in 1976. Compared to other activist video groups operating outside of London in the 1970s – notably in Sheffield, Cardiff, Glasgow and Belfast – Manchester Film and Video Workshop had a particularly large collection of video equipment:

> two black and white portapaks, associated mains edit decks, a pair of old black-and-white studio cameras (which could be linked with the portapack cameras to provide multi-camera coverage of an event), TV sets and two home video cassette recorders.[18]

However, the majority of this equipment was out of date compared to what was available on the market at the time. This highlights the scarcity of funding and support for even the most well-equipped activist video groups outside of the South-East, and is evidence of the imbalance of video work taking place between the South-East and elsewhere.

Manchester Film and Video Workshop initially functioned in a similar way to insider groups such as Graft On!, Albany Video and West London Media Workshop, providing access to video and editing equipment for local groups and individuals struggling to access their own means of representation. Greg Dropkin, an American photographer and political activist, joined the Workshop in 1978. Dropkin lived locally, and brought with him previous experience using portable video as an instrument for agitation, change and reportage. Between 1978 and 1979 the Workshop collaborated with 107

Right and below:
Manchester Film and Video Workshop at work, from publication *Street Video* (1980).

different local activist and community organisations. 'I'm not trying to make "my" films,' said Dropkin, 'In work I've done there have been a lot of people involved at different levels... I'm not concerned to override what other people may want – although I'll put my point across.'[19]

One long-term video project, *Immigration and Deportation* (1980), usefully illustrates Manchester Film and Video Workshop's hybrid approach. The project began after a discussion screening of a video exploring the attempted deportation of a local resident in Oldham. The video functioned very much like a trigger film, and subsequently two audience members – a community advice worker and a law centre worker who lived nearby – approached Workshop members with the idea of making a similar video together. After a number of meetings, several more local residents had joined the project. The aim was to produce a 'comprehensive, informed and watchable video tape' that would make a significant contribution to activist campaigns opposing repressive and racist immigration laws. The project engaged directly with street-level protests while, at the same time, the protesters were actively engaged with the Workshop:

> A picket of the immigration appeals office in Manchester to support Pakistani Nasira Begum was covered by Greg Dropkin and Bob Jones from the workshop with a Portapak ... The 50 or so people on the demonstration mostly know of the film and video workshop already and are more than willing to cooperate and be interviewed.[20]

The make-up of the group allowed for critical and informed discussions about both the content of the video and its potential audience. The Workshop staff were embedded in the community but had no direct experience of these aggressive policies, while the local residents involved in the project had first-hand experience at the sharp end of the law, but lacked video production experience. The collaboration resulted in a multi-directional and horizontal exchange of ideas; research and production tasks were divided up between the group depending on availability and experience, with everyone having equal input on the direction and shape of the project. As local campaigns developed to challenge racialised deportation proceedings, arrangements and training were organised so as many of these events as possible could be recorded with video Portapaks. The hybrid position of the Workshop staff made it easy for them to attend these events, gain the trust of the people at the demonstrations and collect interview material. Unlike the approaches used to produce programmes for television, the Workshop's approach centred discussion and consultation to work 'jointly with groups towards a mutually agreed production ... [while] trying to break down the myth and elitism of media technology.'[21]

Unfortunately, none of the original video materials remain, but the project was included in the publication *Street Video*, a 1980 study of five activist video groups outside of London, based in Sheffield, Cardiff, Glasgow, Belfast as well as Manchester. As was common in 'hybrid' community video projects, members of Manchester Film and Video Workshop functioned as mediators between the 'outside' processes – that is, activist video production – and the 'inside' group of activists. As embedded video practitioners, Dropkin and his colleagues understood the potential and capacity of video production; as local residents, they were able to engage responsively with the participants and mediate the relationship between them and their intended audience,

Manchester Film and Video Workshop at work, from *Street Video* (1980).

Inter-Action at work (1970s).

marshalling their understanding and use of video to meet collective aims. As a relatively invisible and under-represented group, the activists were able to consider and control how they themselves wanted to be represented and to decide what to include or edit out. The participants, starting as subjects in front of the camera, increasingly took on the role of the outsiders – as video- and decision-makers behind the camera. This complex relationship, with its multiple levels of accountability, makes itself manifest in what is *not* shown, in the careful sharing of processes of production, as much as in what is seen in the finished videos.

The specific processes used to produce activist videos are reconfigured each time a project is initiated. They are always contingent on the make-up of the participants involved and the content and intentions of the video they set out to make. The contingency and shared authorship of activist video projects meant that funding bodies often perceived them as social work rather than moving image productions, while arts organisations dismissed them for not conforming to preconceived aesthetics and modes of moving image production. By the end of the 1970s, activist video projects were criticised by some for placing too much emphasis on 'process' while having little regard for producing a finished video.[22] One 1977 report, citing the 'shortage of completed tapes of viewable quality', complained that video was, in the hands of activists, 'easy to use badly and difficult to use well.'[23] Such critiques, however, fail to recognise that an emphasis on process and a disregard for aesthetic orthodoxies are defining factors of activist videos.

The participants of early insider activist video projects were able to draw on the grassroots political movements emerging within the neighbourhoods where they were based to produce and share videos that were representative of the experiences and concerns of those involved. Those videos speak on behalf of the collectives they were part of, whether a tenants association demanding a change to their rights, a childcare group proposing a new system of funding or a community protesting against mistreatment. It was possible for these groups to develop long-term, sustainable and responsive projects, dictated by the specific needs of communities.

Outsider activist video projects attempt to create a space where individuals can share their collective experience of a given issue, for example a problem with traffic in a built-up area, the provision of after-school activities, or the treatment of a particular social or political moment. Finally, hybrid activist video projects begin with a structure that is able change iteratively, inviting participants to navigate and choose how they engage with the project. The formulation of these hybrid projects is based on the individual needs and experiences of the participants.

Video activism started to happen in the early 1970s, with the introduction of a theoretical framework that saw video being used by community groups at a local level for grassroots activism. This was a departure from the filmmaking approaches that preceded this moment; Liberation Films' *Starting to Happen* shows us a mode of moving image production that was profoundly and politically committed, focused *and* practical. Video activism was developing at ground level, through iterative processes based on collaboratively negotiating and learning by experience, testing methodologies, developing theory and praxis in parallel and then applying this in the context of the specific needs of a particular community to confront the issues it was facing. At the same time, the practice was actively securing its own future by embedding skills and encouraging participants to continue to make video activist projects long after the original facilitators might have moved on.

Due to the responsive and contingent nature of activist video processes, any kind of repetition or direct transposition of these is impossible. However, they continue to offer a means of production that is adapted, updated and modified according to and reflective of the specific time and place they are being carried out. Early portable video technology encouraged pre-existing groups to develop their own forms of self-representation and allowed for activist and campaign groups to involve those impacted and ignored by those in power in processes of collective self-representation.

As the 1970s gave way to the 1980s, however, the context shifted, along with the content and themes explored. Video activism expand its reach beyond local issues to include concerns of identity and experience, including race, gender and sexuality. With each shift, the specificity of video continues to engender collaboration and experimentation for video activists, while the specific processes developed by these groups remain reflective of the politics and experiences of the participants involved.

Close-up: Inter-Action and the Media Van

> You could do theatre on the roof, and you could do back-projection films through the back, you could do video out the side, and we had portable video equipment to roam around ... The Media Van was a much more compact and more cost-effective way of going into communities, getting them to use video, to see things that they hadn't seen before.
>
> from *The Resistible Rise of Video Culture*, 1978 [24]

Portable video took on a whole new meaning in the early 1970s with the arrival of Inter-Action's 'Media Van'. The film *Inter-Action Media Van* (1974) documents its arrival in a Newcastle neighbourhood to explain how to introduce portable video technology to 'a tenants association and youngsters in a park' as a means to engage people from different backgrounds in the production of a video about issues facing their neighbourhood.

Inter-Action developed from a street theatre troupe established by the American-born social activist ED Berman (whose other innovations include the 'city farm') and went on to include a community centre, a film and video department and a community art bus. Their work also helps to frame the development of activist video in the context of the emerging community arts movement. Like the Arts Labs, Berman was exploring ideas around 'space, the environment, media and the relationship to the audience',[25] alongside what he called the 'interactive games method.'[26] This process involved developing simple collaborative games to build groups and create shared experiences between participants.

In the opening scene of *Inter-Action Media Van*, a camera fixed to the outside of the van is shown directly transmitting video onto television screens mounted on one side of the vehicle. Participants are able to see themselves as one large group and then, as the camera pans and zooms in, as individuals who wave and gesticulate back at the camera. Regardless of their age, they appear like young children seeing themselves in a mirror for the first time. Inter-Action video projects often started in this way, with a live feed between the camera and a monitor so that participants could instantly see themselves 'on TV'. This was based on the understanding that only once participants had used the technology themselves would they 'be willing to be the subject of a video – to see themselves.'[27]

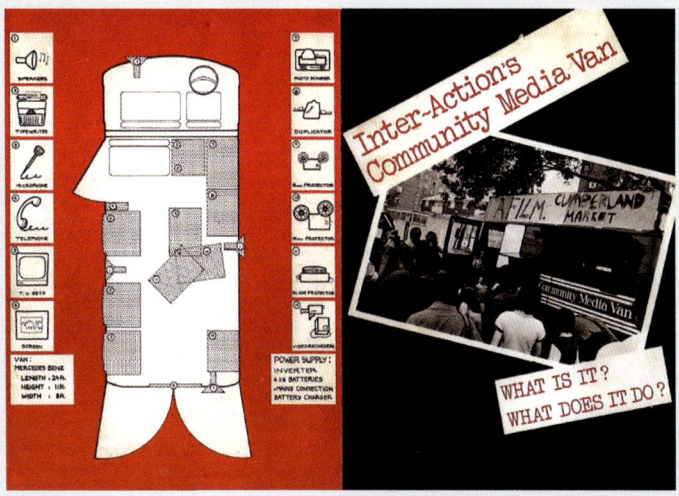

Inter-Action leaflet (c. 1974).

When this introductory game has drawn a large enough crowd of interested participants, they are divided into three small groups. One group arrange themselves to receive camera training from an Inter-Action facilitator: 'Let's all just sit around in a circle and see how this works shall we? I want an agreement between us that if I say how to use it, you will all use it properly ... this is a video portapak ...'

The man hands the camera over to the children, aged around 10 or 11, showing them how to use the zoom and the record buttons. The group very quickly begin using it themselves and the man disappears from the shot: having begun as the holder of the camera, then become an instructor in its use, he ends up only a voice from behind the camera. Finally, as the young people pass the camera around to teach one another, the facilitator disappears altogether and the voices of the young participants replace his voice. A second group of young people, also sat in a circle, make lists on large sheets of paper. Collectively, they suggest themes for a possible video, with prompts from another facilitator. The third group, meanwhile, is invited to draw up a storyboard in the style of a comic strip so that they can plan the order and content of the shots they will later record on video.

The action is centred on rapid learning through playing with the technology. There is minimal direct instruction from the facilitators; instead, their focus is on creating a space where participants learn about and try out the various features of video cameras together. The video ends with the groups watching back the footage they have recorded and then discussing how, as a neighbourhood, they might use the technology in the future.

5. THE PEOPLE'S ACCOUNT

'Don't Film Us! Film the Police!' urged one demonstrator's placard at a Black Lives Matter protest in London in June 2020. It was a reminder to fellow demonstrators of the need to monitor those in power. A year later, the Know Your Rights group, set up to support Black youth being racially profiled by police in Britain, posted on its Instagram account a guide on 'filming the police in relation to stop and search arrests'. In six slides, it outlines why and how to record police behaviour, as well as how to distribute this footage to police accountability organisations such as Y-Stop, Release UK and Stopwatch.

Both the placard and the guide highlight the continuing role of video activism not only as a form of self-representation, but also as a means of self-defence, holding authority to account and presenting otherwise hidden truths. This approach, originating in the 1970s and 1980s, uses video to insist, 'This is not fiction; this is fact; I was there.' This declaration, by Arthur Lawrence, a member of the West Indian Leadership Council, features in *The People's Account*, a 1985 activist video by Ceddo Film and Video Workshop, which presents a grassroots view of events that exposed racialised police violence in London in the 1980s.

Two earlier activist videos, *Aug 13: What Happened?* and *Who Killed Colin Roach?*, delivered similar investigations into racist violence and subsequent uprisings, with first-person accounts from those involved. The titles of both videos function as demands to which each seeks to respond. The first, made by Albany Video in 1977, follows clashes in South East London between anti-fascist groups and both the police and the far-right National Front. The second, made in 1983 by Isaac Julien, charts the aftermath of the

Who Killed Colin Roach? (Isaac Julien, 1983).

death of a Black 23-year-old who died in the entrance of a police station in Stoke Newington, North London, close to where Julien lived. The filmmakers of all three video projects were directly affected by the actions they recorded. Their objectives lay somewhere between the forensic and the personal: an attempt to provide a counter-position to the racist narrative being perpetuated at the time by the police and mainstream media.

The conflict between Black British people and the police depicted and investigated in these videos can be traced back as far as 1919. Following the First World War, an apparent surplus in the labour force led to discontent among Britain's white working class, in particular seamen, who blamed a lack of jobs and homes on African, Afro-Caribbean, Chinese, Arab and South Asian residents. In a number of port towns between January and August that year, a series of racially motivated attacks and police raids on the homes of minority groups resulted in five fatalities. In the late 1950s, following prolonged fascist organising by groups such as the White Defence League and Oswald Mosley's Union Movement, similar clashes took place in Notting

Aug 13th: What Happened? (Albany Video, 1977).

Hill, West London. A week of disturbances in the neighbourhood in August 1958 was sparked by ongoing racism against the increased presence of Afro-Caribbeans of what is now called the 'Windrush generation'. Twenty years later little appeared to have changed. In a 1978 interview for Granada Television's *World in Action*, the then Conservative Party leader Margaret Thatcher complained that 'people are really rather afraid that this country might be rather swamped by people with a different culture.'[1]

Aug 13: What Happened?, produced a few months before Thatcher's now infamous comments, is an early demonstration of the dynamic and forensic way video could be used to represent a group experiencing racist treatment from far-right groups and the police. The video traces the experiences of a community impacted by a 1977 National Front (NF) march through their South East London neighbourhood. Like the actions of racist groups in Notting Hill in the 1950s, the march was part of a wider campaign to target traditionally white working-class areas and provoke residents to feel threatened by the number of Black and Asian people living in their neighbourhoods. The All-Lewisham Campaign against Racism and Fascism had approached Albany Video to act as witnesses and document the NF march as well as the Campaign's own anti-fascist counter-march. The resulting video begins with a unifying speech by the Bishop of Southwark addressed to to the anti-fascist protesters in Ladywell Fields before the march. This is followed by images of the NF march being escorted through the area of New Cross by police. The video goes into detail, tracking how the NF marchers were mismanaged by the police, leading to clashes with anti-fascist groups and, later, between demonstrators and the police. It also shows the first time police deployed riot gear on the UK mainland and provides vital evidence about the demonstration and its aftermath, in which over 100 people were injured.

The form of the video is both analytical and personal, combining testimony from multiple eyewitnesses, often contradicting official reports, with footage recorded before, during and after the events. It is divided into three parts which collectively attempt to piece together what really happened: documentation of the march and its violent aftermath, captured by three or four video cameras; video recordings and photography shot by local community members who were also part of the action; and interviews with participants after the action took place. The video was distributed on VHS to anti-racist groups through Albany Video's distribution catalogue. Both the making of the video and subsequent screenings provided important opportunities for local residents directly impacted by the march and its aftereffects to be shared and heard.

Mounting police harassment of Black communities came to an explosive head in the early 1980s. In April 1981, as part of the provocatively-named 'Operation Swamp', the Metropolitan Police carried out a reported 943 'stop and search'[2] cases in Brixton, South London, most of them targeting Black youth. This aggressive racial profiling resulted in a weekend of demonstrations and violent clashes between local residents and the police. A few months later, on 3 July 1981 in Toxteth, Liverpool, a young Black man, Leroy Cooper, was witnessed being violently arrested. For the next nine days the public responded in fury, with fierce confrontations with police on the streets. CS gas grenades, previously deployed by British armed forces in Northern Ireland, were used for the first time by police in mainland Britain. Over the

Aug 13th: What Happened? (Albany Video, 1977).

next few weeks, further unrest followed in Birmingham, Leeds, Manchester and several other British cities. The iconography of the summer, screening night after night in television news and current affairs programmes, was a landscape of ravaged streets, projectile-throwing youths, blazing vehicles and injured police officers – images that returned as the decade went on, both in the context of fresh outbreaks of unrest or in archive footage. Viewers were repeatedly shown imagery linking Blackness to anger, violence and lawlessness, with a vocabulary to match: young Black people were routinely described as 'rioters', 'hooligans' or 'gangs', while the underlying causes of their anger went largely unaddressed. While contemporary media reports and later historical memory invariably describe the unrest as 'riots', the communities involved have typically referred to them as 'uprisings'.

As a response to this, video activists began to document their own experiences, looking to video as a reliable and authentic witness. They were able to make use of newer, more portable and affordable video cameras, which

Aug 13th: What Happened? (Albany Video, 1977).

could record in colour, and sophisticated editing equipment. If it looked and sounded like the TV, perhaps it could challenge what was being shown on the TV, and, with the launch of the Workshop Declaration and Channel 4 in 1982, it might even get a chance to be seen on it.

The Workshop Declaration, which operated between 1982 and 1989, was the result of an agreement between the newly-established Channel 4 and the Association of Cinematograph, Television and Allied Technicians (ACTT) trade union, to support a new models of film and television production, outside of and independent from the previous 'closed shop' of the unionised film and television sector. The Declaration followed a consultation process involving the Independent Filmmakers' Association, the British Film Institute and a number of regional arts organisations, and followed in the line of a number of experimental and politically Left organisations including the Arts Labs and the London Film-makers' Co-operative. It was responsible for supporting the spread of activist video production outside of London, while at the same

The People's Account
(Milton Bryan/Ceddo
Film & Video, 1985).

time diversifying the way videos were made and how they looked. Workshops were required by the Declaration to operate according to a model of 'integrated practice': this meant that alongside the production of films and programmes for television they had also to include distribution, educational activities and increased access to film and video equipment as part of their work. In line with the activist video groups that preceded it, the Declaration included a remit that 'participating groups should be drawn from outside the mainstream film and television sector, with a particular focus on ethnic diversity and a commitment to local issues.'[3]

The Declaration provided a structure for film and videomakers previously excluded from television production. Channel 4, which was publicly owned and commercially funded, was established with a remit to support 'distinctive programming', on which basis it provided funding and a platform for activist video groups to have their videos broadcast. These two initiatives led to the formation of over 100 groups in the form of franchised workshops, whose integrated moving image practices sought to directly address the misrepresentation of minority groups and the lack of representation of diverse experiences on broadcast television. Channel 4 offered franchised workshops contracts of between one and three years, while non-franchised workshops received development funding, resource funding or direct project funding.

A number of these workshops had a specific focus on representing Black and Asian experiences. These included Black Audio Film Collective (formed 1982), Ceddo Film and Video Workshop (1982), Sankofa Film and Video Collective (1983) and Retake (1984), all based in London; and, later, Liverpool Black Media Group and Black WITCH, an offshoot of WITCH (Women's IndependenT Cinema House) in Liverpool (1985). These groups did not exclusively use video; indeed, many preferred to work with 16mm film, which they then transferred onto video for editing and distribution. However, video continued to play an important role in production, and for many underrepresented and misrepresented groups it provided a gateway to the celluloid previously only accessible to white filmmakers. For Ceddo member Menelik Shabazz, 'PortaPak was ... the boat that took me across the ocean into the film world, because without that PortaPak I would not have thought about the possibility of shooting anything.'[4] For others, video offered a new visual language and a mode of self-representation untainted by dominant white filmmakers. June Givanni, a film curator and founder of the Pan African Cinema Archive,

Handsworth Songs (John Akomfrah/Black Audio Film Collective, 1986).

Pressure (Horace Ové, 1975).

went as far as listing being 'shot on video' as one of the key features that characterised Black British film at the time, alongside short durations and a tendency toward documentary forms. These, she notes, were also signifiers of its remaining 'minor' and underfunded.[5]

In response to the ongoing unrest and to demands from within communities experiencing social exclusion, the government began investing in cultural provision, funding community centres and the arts.[6] The Scarman Report, commissioned in the wake of the April 1981 Brixton uprising and published the following November, identified widespread alienation and the impact of material inequality as the root causes of ongoing racial tensions, and also suggested increased cultural provision to reduce societal conflict. A year later, in 1982, the Greater London Council sponsored a conference to re-evaluate access to media production for Black artists, who remained seriously underfunded, despite Channel 4's remit to increase access to camera training and production opportunities for marginalised groups. Meanwhile, white filmmakers and producers continued to be handed responsibility for representing Black issues to the public.[7] 'Black people [need] to become the subjects, rather than merely objects, of the camera,' argued Imruh Caesar, who was associated with Ceddo and the independent production company Kuumba Productions.[8] On the rare occasions that Black and global majority filmmakers did receive funding and support, this tended to be for the production of films that responded to a white gaze, with a focus on presenting 'positive images', and with race relations providing the central narrative drive. In the earlier films of Black British directors Lionel Ngakane, Horace Ové and Menelik Shabazz, the complexities of Black identity in terms of gender and sexuality often remained unexplored, and there was a reliance on realism rather than experimentation in form. Ové made this clear in 1987:

> Here in England there is a danger, if you are black, that all you are allowed to make is films about black people and their problems. White filmmakers on the other hand, have a right to make films about whatever they like.[9]

Reflecting on this period, cultural theorist Stuart Hall describes what Black filmmakers experienced as the 'burden of representation': the pressure to speak for the Black community as a whole and 'the sense of urgency to say it all'.[10] Hall was part of the emerging field of cultural studies, alongside notable cultural theorists Kobena Mercer, Homi K. Bhabha, Paul Gilroy and Gilane Tawadros. Together, their work offered renewed perspectives on the postcolonial subject that interrogated what had previously remained largely unquestioned assumptions around histories of race and its representation. The emergence of cultural studies in the 1980s provided a new theoretical framework and critical context for the production and reception of activist videos that centred Black British lives. With this increased attention and the opportunities that came with it, the marginalised groups that so many activist video projects in the 1970s had sought to 'enable' and 'facilitate' could at last begin doing this work for themselves. Andy Porter, a founding member of the West London Media Workshop (WLMW), describes the shift in the 1980s away from a local-based activism and towards videos made along the lines of identity:

The People's Account (Milton Bryan/Ceddo Film & Video, 1985).

> Our work in WLMW was predicated on the servicing, in some way, of local 'activism' – both as instigators and followers. When these 'movements' died down, so did one strand of the work, and hence the movement into identity politics, responding politically to that new kind of activism.[11]

In the mid-1980s Isaac Julien started making videos exemplifying this new intersectional direction for activist video. Working both individually and collectively to explore and represent his experiences as a young, Black, gay, working-class man, Julien combined documentary aesthetics with an experimental approach to locate himself behind the camera as a filmmaker, and in front of it as an 'artily dressed', 'tender' 'Black youth'.[12] Julien first encountered political filmmaking on a film project made by members of Big Flame, an activist group formed in 1973 and based in his neighbourhood in East London.

Big Flame's members Alan Hayling and Noreen MacDowell were involved with the Newsreel Collective and had previously made films about the Ford Motor Car disputes in Dagenham. In 1982, Julien was involved in *True Romance*, a Newsreel production about teenage relationships made by Big Flame. This was a formative experience for Julien, who took part on both sides of the camera:

> I was involved in some aspects of filming, or I was sort of in a way observing and seeing how different activities were sort of evolving behind the camera. And so that's where my whole interest behind the camera developed.[13]

While studying art at Central St Martin's, Julien drew on these experiences to start making his first video, *Who Killed Colin Roach?* Roach was a 21-year-old Black British man who died on 12 January 1983 as a result of a fatal gunshot wound after having entered the reception of Stoke Newington police station to respond to allegations concerning a theft some days earlier. A subsequent inquest ruled Roach's death a suicide, concluding that he used a shotgun smuggled in with him as he entered the police station. The evidence, however, raised serious doubts. The incident took place amid rising public concerns around policing in the area, where both Julien and Roach lived, with allegations from Hackney Black People's Association that there existed a culture of police brutality, racial harassment, wrongful detention of Black people and racially motivated 'stop and search'.[14] Allegations of a police cover-up followed the inquest, and the case became a locus for civil rights campaigners and Black community groups. Rising tensions between residents and police resulted in protests demanding justice for Roach and his

Who Killed Colin Roach? (Isaac Julien, 1983).

Who Killed Colin Roach? (Isaac Julien, 1983).

family. Julien first became involved in the campaign during these protests. For Julien, Roach could have easily been himself or his brother; the older West Indian women and men marching could have been members of his family. This realisation was the spur to make a video that would continue to question who was responsible for Roach's death and to surveil and expose those in power, as well as provide a platform for those who felt powerless.

In a similar vein to the forensic-cum-personal approach instigated by the makers of *Aug 13: What Happened?*, Julien investigates the murder of Roach and the subsequent protests in the context of wider mistrust of the police. *Who Killed Colin Roach?* offered Julien an opportunity to reflect on certain fixed ways of looking at Black culture, as well as to make space for people experiencing racism to account for how it impacted them. Julien's understanding of video as a means to create counternarratives to those put forward by the police prefigured the contemporary and ubiquitous use of smart phones to monitor police misconduct and abuse of power:

it was really very much about the idea of the camera as this sort of weapon but a weapon that could be used by both sides, because at that time I was very aware that the media being in a way non neutral. Any side could have the camera and then they could tell their version of events. On the whole the version of events I got told was usually from the dominant media. It was very much the police's point of view. So it felt really important make a work that would be seen from the family's point of view.¹⁵

Who Killed Colin Roach? reworks the documentary form to articulate contemporary voices and provides an example of the new direction of activist video, while Julien's access to and subsequent use of video place it in the lineage of earlier activist videos and community video groups: in the credits, Julien thanks community video groups including Oval Video, Albany Video and Fantasy Factory. It's also clear that Julien adapted earlier modes of video activism in the pursuit of new forms of self-representation. For community videomaker Tony Dowmunt, Julien's approach represented a shift from the activist videos made in 1970s:

A Tribute to Black Women (They Don't Get a Chance) (Ann Carney & Barbara Phillips/ Black Women's Media Project & WITCH, 1986)

It feels like it's both very political and very community orientated … but also it is kind of aesthetically adventurous. It felt like it changed the language in some sense of agitating filmmaking and community filmmaking.[16]

Thirty-five years later, Julien recalled: 'I felt it would be important to document [the demonstration], and at least try to make a work which could be used by his [Roach's] family.'[17] Here, Julien draws out not only the importance of holding up a mirror to injustice, but also the way this documentation can be used to challenge and perhaps change the circumstances that brought about that injustice.

Following the production of *Who Killed Colin Roach?*, Julien, with the support of the Workshop Declaration and Channel 4, co-founded Sankofa Film and Video Workshop with Martina Attille, Maureen Blackwood, Nadine Marsh-Edwards and Robert Crusz. Alongside similar groups, including Black Audio Film Collective, Retake, Ceddo, Liverpool Black Media Group and Black WITCH, Sankofa would forge new approaches to film and video activism, carving out space for the voices and experiences of Black British subjects to be heard and shared. Unlike previous Black filmmakers, they were not satisfied with presenting 'positive images'; rather, the films and videos made by these groups were anti-assimilationist and centred on 'polyvocal' investigations of Black identity within the British experience, intersecting along lines of gender, sexuality and class. Reflecting on the impact of these contemporary forms of moving image production, and contrary to Thatcher's framing of minority groups at the start of the decade, the cultural theorist Kobena Mercer and Isaac Julien wrote:

> The initial stage in any deconstructive project must be to examine and undermine the force of the binary relation that produces the marginal as a consequence of the authority invested in the center.[18]

To represent the voices of marginalised, misrepresented and ignored groups, the production processes used by these collectives echoed those of earlier community and activist video projects, adopting non-hierarchical methods of organisation and shared authorship. However, following the Workshop Declaration, members of these groups often chose to be credited as indi-

Handsworth Songs (John Akomfrah / Black Audio Film Collective, 1986).

vidual directors and, as Julien's hybrid approach demonstrates, the aesthetic of their finished videos marked a departure from what had come before. Acknowledging the influence of documentary pioneer John Grierson, Black Audio Film Collective's Reece Auguiste noted that BAFC's *Handsworth Songs* (1986), about uprisings against the police in Birmingham, was made in a 'Grierson spirit with our own diasporic inflection adding substance to it,'[19] an approach that allowed 'space to deconstruct the hegemonic voices of British television newsreels.'[20]

Julien and his contemporaries took advantage of innovations in colour video and advances in editing technology to create their own 'cut and paste' aesthetic inspired by the underground 'scratch video' movement. Exponents of scratch video were as influenced by music video culture as they were by documentary forms. Their work combined home video recording equipment with new 'vision-mix' editing technology, which allowed several different live video sources to be edited together. Videomakers could create montages featuring archival materials and add visual effects such as on-screen text, freeze-frames, slow motion and even rudimentary greenscreen to enable cutouts and superimposition. Early scratch video exponent and video activist Mark Saunders recalls recording material from the television onto VHS and reworking it,

> using cut-ups and archive stuff taken from TV, re-filming photographs and images ... taking a bit of Thatcher's speech and changing a few words, so that she says what she probably means but dare not say.[21]

This experimental editing style combined 'surrealism, jump cuts, comedy, repetition and documentary modes' – characteristics more commonly found in music videos of the time.[22] All of this served to hold the attention of the audience on specific, intimate and personal moments and created a new visual language suited to the subject matter; one that transgressed the one-directional flow of broadcast television. In a 1984 article, Andy Lipman, then the video editor at the alternative listings magazine *City Limits*, explained the origins of scratch video and the processes it entailed:

> Broadcast TV is scoured for arresting images and fed into video editing systems like shredding machines. The fusion of funk rhythms and visuals on collision course crumble original context. Reassurance and sweet reason, television's facade, disintegrate before your bombarded eyes ...What emerges isn't just a jumble of voices and images but the personality of broadcast TV itself. Its self-importance, its hectoring, its banality and plastic smile.[23]

The reclamation of found-footage from archives and news broadcasts would also become a touchstone for Black filmmakers seeking to write, re-write and amend their misrepresentation, as Isaac Julien remembers:

> video activism and music and politics ... could come together in video-making, which was a kind of form of making protest works but ... [was] very much infused with the language of the rock promo culture or Video FX in their infancy.[24]

The convergence of art school, cultural studies and earlier approaches to activist film and video production gave rise to a new confidence among

Step Forward Youth (Menelik Shabazz, 1977).

Black artists and forged a language that subsequent generations of artists and activists could take ownership of and continue to build on. Menelik Shabazz, who would go on to make *People's Account* in 1985, described his introduction and approach to videomaking as being both inspired by and in opposition to earlier activist video groups. Much like Isaac Julien and his work with Big Flame, Shabazz was introduced to video by his local community arts group, Inter-Action, who gave a class at his college on how to use a Portapak video camera. He remembers: 'I immediately had an idea and I got a group of people together, and we just said okay, went off and started shooting stuff and I was like, "wow I like this".'[25] Although drawn to the technology, his understanding of the subjects about which he wanted to make videos led him to develop his own, more traditional approach to production:

Breaking Point (Menelik Shabazz, ITV tx 19/12/1978).

> I didn't want to do it in the style that they were working in, because at that time it was very much about demystifying cinema and documentary ... I wanted to shoot a little bit more static, I didn't want all this moving around because the people that I was aiming it for are not going to be au fait with that more avant garde style.[26]

In 1977, Shabazz made his first film, *Step Forward Youth*. Shot on 16mm film, it documented the experiences of Black youth in London. Situating itself within the broader lineage of activist and oppositional filmmaking, *Step Forward Youth* was distributed by independent, radical left organisation The Other Cinema, formed in the 1970s, and it was following a screening at the London Film-makers' Co-op (who once shared a building with the early video workshop TVX) that Shabazz was invited by Birmingham based broadcaster ATV to make a programme for television. In 1978, he proposed and started making *Breaking Point*, a documentary about the so-called 'Sus' laws, which empowered the police to arrest any 'suspected person or reputed thief ... with intent to commit an arrestable offence' and was heavily used by the police at the time, largely to criminalise young Black men and women. 'I was happy as a lark,' remembered Shabazz, 'I'd reached the mainstream – life was good! I didn't realise the stir I was causing in this exclusive white world.'[27] What was different and perhaps revolutionary about *Breaking Point* was that it was the first documentary made for mainstream television in which all the people talking in authority positions were Black, among them Stuart Hall, Yehudi Narayan and Paul Boateng. Problems arose during the post-production phase, when the regulatory body the Independent Broadcast Authority (IBA) objected to the cut, complaining that it was too biased in favour of the Black experience. Shabazz argued that it was 'counter-balancing the one-sided media approach to Black youth issues.'[28] The film was ultimately broadcast after ITV's *News at Ten* in 1978, but only under the proviso that it was preceded by a statement that would satisfy the regulator and deflect any possible pushback away from the broadcaster. The statement read 'This film is made by a black director, it's about people's feelings.' At a time when there were still only three channels, *Breaking Point* was viewed by millions, contributing to the momentous repeal of the Sus laws three years later in 1981. The response brought home to Shabazz the power of television: 'I always felt that if the mainstream was able to work for the benefits of the people and ideas, and to be expansive, then it would be such a great vehicle.'[29] But the experience also made him realise that he was 'a rebel soul and working in mainstream TV was not the way forward.'[30]

Fortunately, the arrival of the Workshop Declaration and Channel 4 provided Shabazz with a more conducive context for the work and ideas he had been developing. Subsequently, he co-founded Ceddo Film and Video Workshop, alongside Milton Bryan, Imruh Bakari, Lazell Daley, Chuma Ukpabi, June Reid, D. Elmina Davis, Glenn Ujebe Masokonane, Vusi Challenger, Sukai Eccleston and Dada Imarogbe. Ceddo's productions made space to critique British society's mistreatment of Black British people and to represent the Black British experience, together with a focus on African and Caribbean politics and history. Ceddo were one of the first organisations to run film courses in and for the Black community, while also screening films and sharing resources with the wider community of Black filmmakers and activists, in line with the emphasis at the time on 'integrated practice'.

The People's Account (Milton Bryan/Ceddo Film & Video, 1985).

Cultural theorist Kobena Mercer describes Ceddo as 'cinematic activists.'[31] The group took their name from the 1977 film by Senegalese director Ousemane Sembène. In the words of Shabazz, 'Ceddo means "cultural resistance", [which] ... typified what we were about. We were trying to tell our stories without filter.'[32] As well as organising video training and outreach projects, and making standalone videos, Ceddo functioned as a guerrilla unit, using video to document demonstrations and protests against police violence in Handsworth, Brixton and Tottenham. Like the Albany Video crew in 1977, they provided a mode of surveillance of the police response to the uprisings.[33] But while *Aug 13: What Happened?* was about racial tensions, the people behind the camera, however sympathetic, were white, with no direct experience of racial prejudice. By the 1980s, the marginalised groups that so many activist video projects had sought to 'enable' and 'facilitate' in the 1970s were able to do this work on their own terms.

In 1985 Ceddo were commissioned by Channel 4 to make *The People's Account*, a record of a community's response to the death of Cynthia Jarrett, a resident of the Broadwater Farm Estate in Tottenham, at the hands of the police. Prior to her death, Cynthia's son, Floyd, had been apprehended by police in north London for driving his car with an expired tax disc. The police suspected the car had been stolen, and subsequently charged him with theft and assault. Later that day, more officers, allegedly looking for Floyd, arrived at his mother's house on the estate and forcefully entered the premises. During the intrusion, Cynthia suffered a fatal heart attack and collapsed. Her death followed just a few years after that of Colin Roach and took place in a climate of fear stirred up by the ongoing ruthless and often brutal treatment of Black people by the police.

The People's Account provided a counternarrative to the often sensationalist media coverage that unquestioningly supported police actions and did little to engage with the communities impacted by them. The processes used by Ceddo during its production were similar to those of previous activist videos; rather than being the authors of an intrusive or moralising story, they used their platform to collaborate with the men, women, families and friends,

The People's Account (Milton Bryan/Ceddo Film & Video, 1985).

The People's Account
(Milton Bryan/Ceddo
Film & Video, 1985).

Who Killed Colin Roach?
(Isaac Julien, 1983).

*Aug 13th: What
Happened?*
(Albany Video, 1977).

who were able to share and communicate their experience of trying to live their lives in the shadow of sustained and oppressive police surveillance and suspicion. The motivation behind the video was close to that driving *Who Killed Colin Roach?* and *Aug 13*: all three were made by people living in the neighbourhood where the production took place. 'I lived across the road from Broadwater Farm. I knew the people. Tottenham was my manor,' explained Shabazz, 'I thought, we need to have a consistent way of documenting our story ... when the Broadwater Farm uprising kicked off we were in the area and it was important that we had to be there.'[34]

The finished 50-minute video uses footage of the press conference marking the publication of the Broadwater Farm enquiry' report, which followed the uprisings ignited by Jarrett's death, alongside interviews with people living on the Estate and impacted by the death and its aftermath. The press release for the video describes it as an examination of the way the media and the police 'distort and undermine the fundamental reasons for the uprisings'. The use of the word 'uprising' was central to Ceddo's understanding of what happened on Broadwater Farm. Rejecting the mainstream media's description of the events as 'rioting', the video frames them as an 'example of self-defence by the [Black] community', and the production of the video can be understood as an extension of this. A voiceover, written by Pan-African activist and scholar Cecil Gutzmore and read by actor and academic Lola Young, ties the different threads and observations together. Alongside documentation of discussions and feedback from local residents, archival materials are used to situate the action in the context of wider social and historical racialised struggles and oppression.

Following completion of *The People's Account* in 1985, Shabazz and Ceddo faced more conflict with the regulator, reinforcing the limits of engagement between activist videomakers and mainstream television production charted throughout this book. This time, the IBA objected to the description of the police in the video as 'racist, lawless terrorists' and to the justification of the uprising on Broadwater as a legitimate act of self-defence. Ceddo refused the changes demanded by the regulator, and the programme was pulled from the schedules. It would never be shown on British television.

The production processes of each of the videos described in this chapter reflect different approaches to activist videomaking as a mode of self-defence in response to racialised police violence and misconduct. *The People's Account* was shot on low-cost colour video, and made collectively for television. Albany Video's *Aug 13: What Happened?* was also collectively made by a community video group, but with no expectation of broadcast. It too follows a fairly traditional format but, because of technological limitations at the time, was shot on black-and-white tape and distributed through local networks and catalogues. *Who Killed Colin Roach?*, however, was made individually by Isaac Julien, using newly-available colour video cameras and sophisticated editing techniques; it includes poetry and music and follows a more artistic, experimental approach, focusing on the personal and rejecting the analytical line employed in the other two videos. Nevertheless, the three productions share a motivation to bear witness and chronicle the impact of racist policing, as well as a common aesthetic and a number of formal similarities that characterise this mode of activist video. By tracing a linear series of events in a matter-of-fact way, all three videos provide nuanced and complex counternarratives that challenge the racist misrepresentation of the experiences of the protagonists by mainstream media at the time. Each video uses archival footage and documentary photography to draw connections between the past and the present, revealing the endemic and ongoing nature of the issues they highlight.

In each of the productions, stony-faced police officers are shown opposing impassioned and articulate demonstrators, who stand together and chant in unison. These images are interspersed with first-person accounts, presented in long, unedited sections, avoiding didactic one-liners. Interviewees are given time and space to explain and describe their experiences in their own words. They are often recorded in pairs or small groups rather than as isolated talking heads, establishing them as part of their community. Each of the videos mimics factual programming, presenting statistics around racialised policing as well as graphics and on-screen text to explain or clarify events. In a significant departure from earlier activist videos, sound – particularly music – plays a key role in setting a tone and shaping the rhythm and flow of the edit. When the soundtrack is not made up of voiceovers, guiding and explaining the events on screen, musical and poetic interludes provide moments of reflection and introduce an engagement that is emotive rather than analytical. These videos map the personal onto the factual and back again.

Hard Stop (George Amponsah, 2015).

In 2017, forty years after it was made, *Aug 13: What Happened?*, long thought to be lost, was rediscovered and shown at a number of commemorative discussion–screening events with the aim of shedding light on allegations of police brutality made at the time. Invited panellists and audience members reflected on the continued importance of anti-fascist organising, as well as the perpetuation of violent and racist police tactics used to control protests and demonstrations. In 2020, meanwhile, Isaac Julien drew links between his own work making *Who Killed Colin Roach?* and the growing Black Lives Matter movement, which surged after bystander video footage bore witness to the violent death of a Black man, George Floyd, during his arrest by police in Minneapolis, Minnesota:

> That we're living in the 21st century and still have these questions of paramount importance just shows you that these things have not improved at all. Thinking about George Floyd, there is a sense that things have gone backwards.[35]

The People's Account has been screened alongside the 2015 documentary *Hard Stop*, which traces the events leading up to and following the death of

Rendering of the moment Mark Duggan steps out of a minicab (Forensic Architecture, 2020).

Mark Duggan, a Black British man who lost his life at the hands of police in 2011. Peaceful protests over the event escalated into several days of unrest around the UK. The circumstances had strong similarities to those documented in *The People's Account*, with both films exploring the consequences of racist policing in Tottenham. As Menelik Shabazz remarked, 'people were able to look at what we did in *The People's Account* and contrast that with *Hard Stop* and Mark Duggan.'[36]

The killing of Mark Duggan was also the subject of an in-depth investigation and report published in 2020 by the multidisciplinary research group Forensic Architecture. The project was commissioned by lawyers for the Duggan family and carried out collectively. Forensic Architecture used cutting-edge technology, including 3D modelling, spatial reconstruction, data mining and virtual reality, to piece together police reports and bystander evidence, including footage recorded on a mobile phone at the scene, to produce a counternarrative challenging official police and media reports. Although the form and technology used to make this new work distinguish it from the activist videos discussed here, the motivations behind and processes involved in its production place it in their lineage. The pioneering work of the first generation of Black video activists testify to the potency of video as a means to expose wrongdoing by those in power and give voice to those suffering its effects, and stands as a model for today's activist groups to chronicle their experiences, hold authorities to account and speak truth to power.

This chapter is dedicated to the life and work of Menelik Shabazz, who passed away while I was writing it.

Close-up: The Miners' Campaign Tapes

The product of a cross-class alliance between miners and progressive media workers, the *Miners' Campaign Tapes* (1984–85) was a series of six videotapes, which brought together activist video networks across the UK to raise awareness and draw support for striking coalminers during the year-long Miners' Strike of 1984–85.

Groups involved included Cinema Action, Platform Films and Films at Work (all based in London); Trade Films (Gateshead); Nottingham Video Project; Open Eye Film and Video Workshop (Liverpool); Chapter Community Video Workshop (Cardiff); Amber Films (Newcastle); Edinburgh Workshop Trust; Birmingham Film and Video Workshop; and Active Image (Rotherham and Sheffield). This consortium built on networks and production processes established and developed in the 1970s, with the object of co-ordinating a nationally-connected activist video project, positioning it historically and methodologically at the nexus of two approaches to video activism.

The Miners' Campaign Tapes (Miners' Campaign Tape Project, 1984).

The strike was ignited by National Coal Board proposals – backed by the Thatcher government – to close 20 'uneconomic' collieries around the UK, cutting 20,000 jobs and robbing many communities of their primary source of employment. The National Union of Mineworkers believed (rightly, as it turned out) that the proposals signalled a much wider closure programme to come.

Unlike previous campaign tapes, which were often made retrospectively, these videos were made to intervene in the present. The tapes needed to be made quickly so as to be useful during the strike. Most were shot on low- or high-band U-Matic 3/4-inch tape, which offered superior recording quality to VHS. But it was VHS technology that made replication and distribution possible. At the height of the *Campaign Tapes* project, 4,000 videos were in circulation, distributed via mail order or by collection in person; they were free to miners, miners' wives and support groups and available to others at a low cost.[37] 'Without video there would have been no project,' acknowledged Chris Reeves of Platform Films, who was instrumental in initiating the project.[38]

The campaign would be, unapologetically, as partisan as the British media, countering what its creators saw as the bias against the strikers revealed in every BBC or ITV report, particularly around representations of police violence. While the strikers were typically represented as violent and unruly, images of police aggression were all-but erased. Tellingly, journalists and TV cameras were almost invariably situated behind the police lines, rather than among the strikers. With rare exceptions, notably Channel Four, the media, said Reeves, were 'abandoning any semblance of impartiality and taking on a propagandist role in support of the state.'[39] In the *Campaign Tapes* video 'The Lie Machine – The Media and the Miners' Strike', a woman relates how a TV camera operator filmed miners pushing police, but turned his camera away when the police attacked the miners. The *Campaign Tapes* presented evidence showing police carrying out unprovoked attacks and deliberately intimidating strikers. The videos also looked beyond the picket lines, interviewing striking miners and highlighting other strike activity, while examining the strike's causes and the way the law operated to constrain the miners' freedom of action.

The finished tapes were shown at union meetings and in public screenings up and down the country – and widely overseas – raising funds and engaging people in the struggle against the pit closures. The project went on to win the prestigious BFI/John Grierson Award in 1985. For critic and film historian Julian Petley, the *Campaign Tapes* revealed

> just how much can be achieved without conventional broadcast media at all. If television consistently ignores or misrepresents those in conflict with the State... then they in turn will increasingly ignore and distrust mainstream television and start looking to the alternatives offered by the new technology.[40]

Montage: Distribution Catalogues

The proliferation of domestic video players through the late 1970s and early 80s put an end to the crude and laborious process of carting a playback deck and monitor around in a pram or in the back of a car. Now activist videos could be shared, like independent films before them, through distribution catalogues. These A4 or A5 paper pamphlets were produced and printed by small community organisations, which, quite often, also made their own activist videos.

Tapes would typically be organised by theme or listed in alphabetical order by title, and include the name of the maker or production company, the country and year of completion and the programme's running time in minutes. Beneath each tape would be a short description of the programme, and in some cases reviews, and a separate comment giving an indication of the programme's intended audience as well as its uses and suitability for different groups.

The catalogues would be posted out to grassroots groups, educational institutions and other collectives or individuals interested in viewing the videos or organising screenings. Tapes would be rented or purchased and then sent out through the post. The cost was often dictated by the scale, budget or aims of the organisation wishing to show the video. Many catalogues would also include advice on organising discussion screenings as well as contact information for other activist video groups and distribution organisations.

Facing page (clockwise from top left): *Liberation Films Distribution Catalogue* (1978); *East End on Screen* (Tower Hamlets Arts Project Books, 1985); *Directory of Video Tape* (London Community Video Workers, 1979); *Cinenova: Catalogue of Films and Videos Directed by Women* (Circles/COW/Cinenova, 1994).

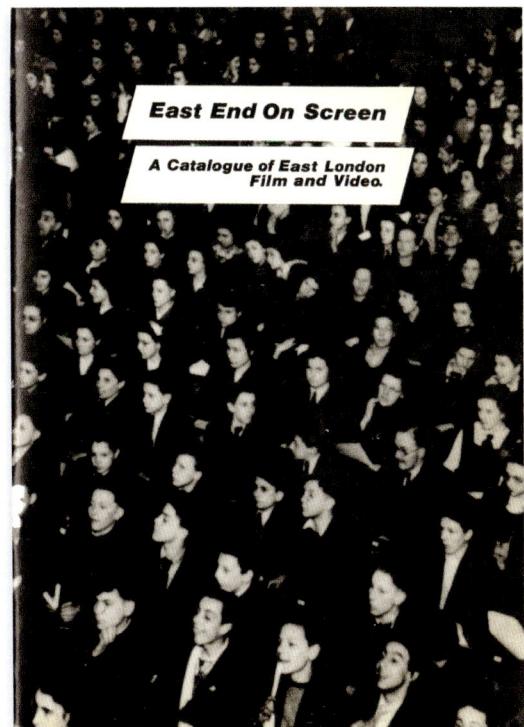

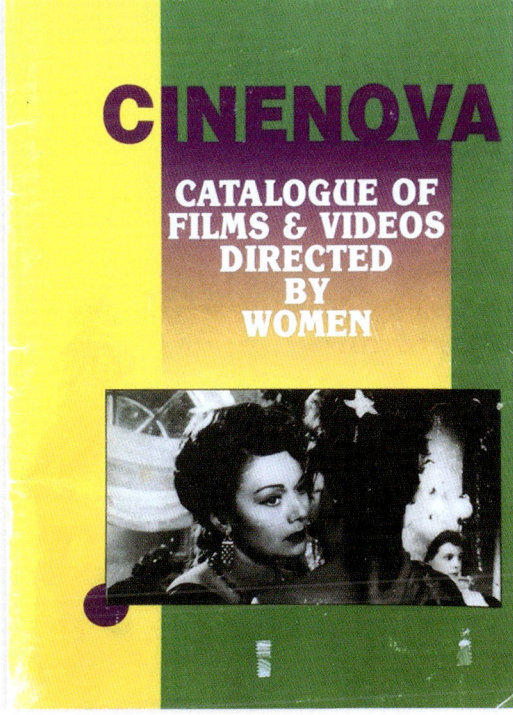

6. GETTING THE WORD OUT

In the 2020s, a video recorded hastily on a smart phone at a protest is shared on Facebook, Snapchat, TikTok, YouTube and Instagram. Viewers send edits and excerpts of the video around -using encrypted messaging apps, and it is reshared online. This use of smartphones and the Internet by activists to get their message out sounds like a very contemporary story. But the intentions and desires of each person pressing 'record', 'send' or 'upload', share much with those of the very first video activists. Activists have long adopted and adapted new communications technology to produce alternatives to mainstream news outlets, build solidarity through screening their videos, told stories and encouraged others to do likewise.

While the earliest, most rudimentary version of the World Wide Web was introduced as early as 1989, it was many years before the Internet would offer a viable distribution platform for video activists. The Internet's promise of free-flowing information was anticipated as early as the late 1960s in the emerging field of cybernetics. The Institute of Contemporary Art's groundbreaking 1968 exhibition 'Cybernetic Serendipity' was the first comprehensive exhibition in Britain devoted to exploring the relationship between new computing technology and the arts. Cybernetics provided video activists with the means to imagine and propose an alternative distribution network, independent of state control, through which they could record and share the latest underground performances, art and political actions. It also offered a framework for understanding the take-up of portable video recording technology in opposition to the one-directional flow of information transmitted by broadcasters and authorities. Instead, video activists were able to propose their own closed-loop communication systems with specific goals that worked iteratively, where, as

Carnival Against Capitalism, 1999.

seen in Cybernetic theories, an action could be understood and improved by its initial effect, then modified and repeated accordingly – a collaborative and responsive approach to production that persists in today's video activism.

In the 1990s and early 2000s, activists continued to draw on the video activism that preceded them, while developing new production methods reflective of the changing social and political situation. What linked these approaches was the urgency for those involved to tell their own stories and control the means of distribution, as well as the continued importance of having an audience in mind from the start. What set them apart was the technology they employed and the shift of the production and reception of their work from the local to the national and, later, the global.

Long before today's joined-up online campaigns, activist groups first started to use the Internet from the early 1990s to communicate with one another via email and through posts on forums, using simple websites to connect campaigns and to coordinate mass actions. Video streaming was still very much in its infancy, and it wasn't until the end of the 1990s

Paul O'Connor in the Small World Media edit suite.

that video activists began to experiment with uploading their videos and streaming them live. In June 1999, undercurrents, an activist media group formed in London, took the global reach of the Carnival against Capitalism, an international day of protest to coincide with the 25th G8 summit in Cologne, to experiment for the first time with live video streaming. Ahead of the summit, undercurrents had been in touch with a DJ and musician who had been experimenting with new Internet connectivity to stream and share his music. undercurrents was part of a larger group of anti-capitalist organisations, co-ordinating video activists who would record what was taking place on the streets. The tapes would then be passed on to bike couriers and transported to an office located close to the action in central London, where they would be transmitted to the rest of the world: 'It was really organised and felt like a military operation,' recalled undercurrents member Paul O'Connor.[1] The aim was to show what was really going on from the perspective of the people involved on the streets, as the protests became a battle between protestors and police in full riot gear. O'Connor goes on to describe what happened next:

Carnival Against Capitalism, 1999.

> We got the tapes back to HQ and went up to the office, where a live DJ set was being streamed. There was so much kit it was like NASA! We loaded up the system to stream the video and were ready and waiting to see how many people would log on and watch. The numbers started to go up, but when we hit the grand number of 30, the bandwidth couldn't handle anymore and it crashed the system. We learnt two valuable lessons that day: we could use the Internet to coordinate a lot of people for one action, but be careful of working with geeks![2]

This example is significant as a reflection not only of the global ambitions of video activists in the late 1990s, but also of the lag between the emergence of new technologies and the capacity of marginalised groups to access and use them. Although the video stream was unreliable, the group was able to share a mixture of pictures, text reports and audio along with similar co-ordinated material gathered from around the world. These were hosted on two websites, J18.org and reclaimthestreets.net.[3] Together, the video activists were able to create a joined-up, real-time picture of grassroots

undercurrents No.1 (undercurrents, 1994).

actions taking place on the same day across over 40 countries, and share it around the world.

Before they had access to the Internet, video activist groups had been focusing their attention on VHS, which, by the early 1980s was, firmly established as the dominant (and ultimately only) domestic video cassette format in the UK and US. Video had always offered self-contained production and exhibition, and with the arrival of VHS it now had easy replication and distribution built in. During the 1980s, video rental shops proliferated on high streets across the UK, while many public libraries offered a similar service. By 1988, a majority of UK households owned or (more commonly) rented a VHS player.[4] In this context, video activists were able to rethink distribution models, anticipating the 'on-demand' availability we now associate with online distribution and video streaming.

In the early 1990s, initiatives like undercurrents and POUT, a video magazine launched in 1992 by a group of queer artists and activists, put VHS

POUT Issue 1 (POUT, 1992).

technology at the heart of their work. The collective behind POUT made the most of their extended friendship networks and links to the arts to produce and eventually distribute their own video magazine in high street shops. undercurrents, meanwhile, borrowed from environmental activists and created media spectacles to build an audience for their material, eventually making use of the Internet to develop a national, and ultimately international production and distribution network. Activist video, as it is understood today, can be traced through these two pioneering activist video collectives, whose collaborative, issue-led and networked approach to production and distribution paved the way for what was to come. The themes and activities covered in the videos made by POUT and undercurrents signaled a change in focus for video activists that reflected wider social-political concerns, with a new emphasis on global struggles and human rights. For POUT, that meant queer activism and LGBTQ representation; for undercurrents, it was anti-capitalism and environmental campaigning.

POUT was both a creative outlet to explore and represent queer life and a response to the lack of video material made by, for and representing the experiences of the queer community. The only visible examples of such content at the time were to be found in Channel 4's programming, notably the magazine series *Out on Tuesday* (later *OUT*, 1989–94) and some editions of the experimental moving image slot *The Eleventh Hour*(1982–89), a late-night strand for more experimental work that also included political and personal documentary, low-budget fiction and perspectives from the Global South, all offering insights into marginalised cultures and politics. It was one *Eleventh Hour* edition – a 1986 screening of the community video project *Framed Youth: Revenge of the Teenage Perverts* – that inspired a group of young lesbians and gays to set about producing what would become POUT.

Framed Youth: Revenge of the Teenage Perverts began as the Lesbian and Gay Youth Video Project in 1982. As Jeff Cole, one of its makers, explains,

> We were challenging the ways that conventional documentary makers were showing lesbians and gay men on television documentaries and so wanted

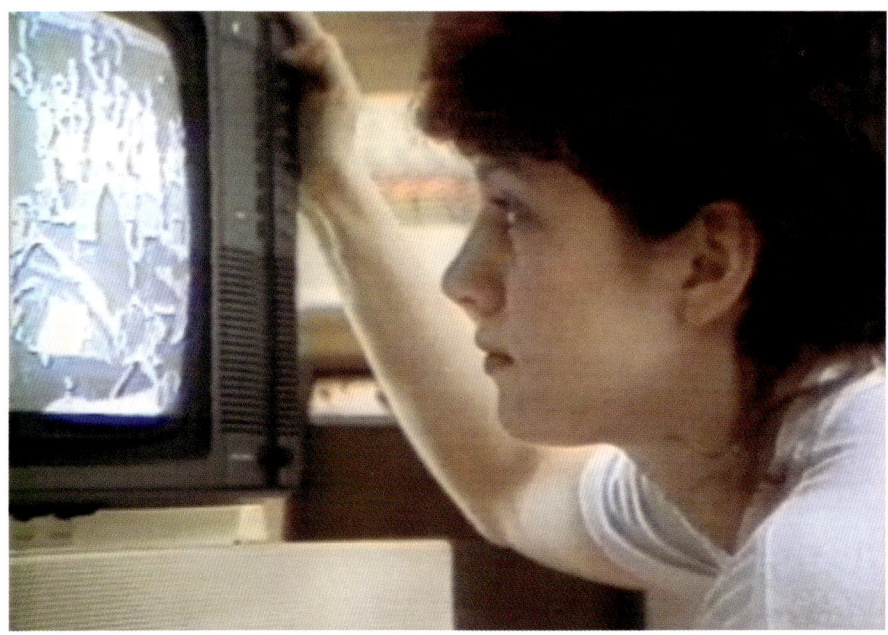

Framed Youth: Revenge of the Teenage Perverts (Lesbian and Gay Youth Video Project, 1983).

to include ourselves as makers and as subjects, not in any way trying to be balanced. We found ways to film each other that helped us feel comfortable and we did loads of experiments using the new VHS and Betamax cameras.[5]

POUT were inspired by the cut-and-paste, experimental, confrontational approach they saw in *Framed Youth*, which had its roots in the alternative theatre group Gay Sweatshop and the scratch video movement. The project was initiated against a backdrop of the mainstream media's continued demonisation of people living with and dying from AIDS, and the passing of the notorious Section 28 of the Local Government Act in 1988, which decreed that:

A local authority shall not –
(a) intentionally promote homosexuality or publish material with the intention of promoting homosexuality;
(b) promote the teaching in any maintained school of the acceptability of homosexuality as a pretended family relationship.[6]

Framed Youth was made by and about a group of young, funny and articulate lesbians and gays from a variety of backgrounds. Watching them reflect on their experiences of coming out, homophobia, romance, sex and sexuality not only encouraged members of POUT to do something similar, it also highlighted how rarely they saw people like themselves on television.

POUT started with a flyer posted around London in 1989, inviting likeminded collaborators to get involved in the production of alternative queer video content. What they ended up making challenged the misrepresentation they were seeing in the media and stuck a proverbial two fingers up at the establishment. POUT was loud, rough, sexy, scrappy and ready to poke fun at anyone who took themselves too seriously. The first POUT meeting took place at Centerprise community bookshop in East London. In attendance were artists, writers, performers and theatre-makers – a similar mix to the makers of *Framed Youth* – including Julie Jenkins, Darren Brady, Andrew Stevens, Amanda Roberts, Tom Abell, Jeffrey Hinton and Mark Harriott; it was a group, in Harriott's words, of 'poor lesbians and gays who wanted to see their lives and stories represented.'[7] The group talked about the absence of any kind of queer material on TV and began to hatch a plan to make their own, drawing on their diverse experience to create the video equivalent of a cabaret show. Harriott was a theatre designer eager to find a platform for work more closely aligned with his experiences. On the bus ride home from that first meeting he continued plotting with Tom Abell, who worked in a post-production facility and was keen to set up his own film and distribution company. This would allow distribution to be built into the project from the outset. Abell was able to make use of his contacts and experience to get the first issue of POUT made and then distribute it in high street shops.

By 1990, one member of POUT, who worked for Camden Council, managed to find a way through the strictures of Section 28 to apply for some funding – enough to buy a VHS-C Panasonic video camera costing over £1000. They also received some support from the BBC's Community Programmes Unit, which, in the early 1990s, invited a small number of groups to use its editing facilities overnight during the studios' downtime. With a new video camera and somewhere to edit their material, POUT started shooting and compiling a mixture of video art performances and magazine features. Members of the group continued to meet monthly, and with an informal network of friends, they extended the invitation out to get more people involved in the production of content for issue one of their new queer video magazine.

While the growing network of collaborators began working on the production of more playful and satirical segments for POUT, others started to attend meetings of the newly-formed queer activist group OUTRAGE! in the basement of the London Lesbian and Gay Centre. OUTRAGE! was established in May 1990 and described themselves as:

> a broad based group of queers committed to radical, non-violent direct action and civil disobedience to: assert the dignity and human rights of queers; fight homophobia, discrimination and violence directed against us; affirm our right to sexual freedom, choice and self-determination.[8]

Much like the motivation behind the Miners' Campaign Tapes, there was a clear need to counter the marginalisation and misrepresentation of

OUTRAGE! Tapes (OUTRAGE!, 1993–94).

OUTRAGE! and its struggles by mainstream media. In their early meetings, members of OUTRAGE! encouraged Mark Harriott to document their demonstrations, which were taking place almost every week. These included actions demanding the equalisation of the age of consent, the 'Stop Murder Music' campaign against homophobic language in popular Dancehall songs of the time, and protests against the Metropolitan Police's use of entrapment against gay men cruising.

Harriott's recordings of these actions have a similar look and feel to videos of miners being manhandled and mistreated by the police. In one sequence, we see protestors lying across a street to stop traffic, arms linked and banners draped over their bodies; others have placards on strings hanging around their necks. The camera pans across the scene and the frame is filled by the arrival of a police van. The cameraperson keeps the camera rolling as he runs, following the action. In the next shot, we see protestors, arms held behind their backs, being dragged off and loaded into the back of the police van.

OUTRAGE Tapes, 1992.

OUTRAGE! employed theatrics to create media spectacles, using eye-catching placards, costumes and large props. They staged mass kiss-ins and a queer wedding, complete with bride and bride in matching wedding dresses. The video documentation of these actions was edited and interspersed between the more experimental and playful clips featured on POUT Issue 1. Mark Harriott recalls one OUTRAGE! caucus called WIG ('Work It Girl'), which focused on queer visibility in London. The result was a short insert, also featured on POUT Issue 1, following members of OUTRAGE! in drag, strutting around London and going into clothing shops, where they asked shop workers what they thought of drag queens and gender non-conforming fashion. By including this material between more light-hearted or sexy clips, POUT presented politics and the work of OUTRAGE! as something accessible, entertaining and even fun: the intention was to politicise people by showing them that activism didn't have to be frightening or violent. By Spring 1992, 1,000 copies of Issue 1 were produced and made available to buy in high street shops.

The video opens with a fast cut edit of shots previewing the different items featured on the tape, set to the 1930s song 'Let's All Be Fairies' by the Durium Dance Band. In the first minute we see leather-clad couples kissing, protestors waving placards saying 'Protection not Seduction', a punk band in fluorescent clothing with a psychedelic greenscreen backdrop, a man in a waistcoat making a trifle, drag queens taking over a shopping mall and scantily-dressed people of all genders dancing wildly. Many of the segments were made for little or no money and were filmed in people's houses or on the sly in shops; props and costumes are obviously handmade, cobbled together with whatever the group could beg, borrow or steal. POUT satirised popular television programmes, from travelogues to celebrity chefs and talent impersonation shows, poking fun at the heteronormativity of mainstream media, while highlighting the lack of queer representation on TV at the time. From the titles alone, it's clear that the POUT collective were always confidently and defiantly queer, with their tongues firmly in their cheeks. POUT came to an end after three issues; in 1992, Mark Harriott and Tom Abell established a film distribution company, Dangerous to Know, producing and distributing VHS tapes and, later, DVDs compiled from LGBTQ+ features, shorts and documentaries found in archives and at film festivals, with the aim of making this hard-to-see work more widely accessible.

POUT Issue 1 (POUT, 1992).

As well as making its post-production facilities available to a number of activist video groups, including POUT, the BBC Community Programmes Unit continued to support the production of community-led programmes with the establishment of the *Video Diaries* series in 1990. The series made use of new HI8 and VHSC camcorders, which, unlike their predecessors, were cheap, light and easy to use, with longer battery life and more stable picture quality. *Video Diaries* followed the CPU's original ethos, with members of the public invited to take part in basic video training before gathering their own material and recording their experiences with a camcorder. Participants would then receive further support in editing and post-production to put together a programme for broadcast on BBC2.

It was a chance viewing of one *Video Diaries* programme, 'Major, the Miners and Me' (tx. 4/9/1993), that set Paul O'Connor on a path to joining the alternative video news project undercurrents. O'Connor was struck by the impact the process of making the video had on protagonist Brenda Dixon, a miner's wife during the strikes against the wave of further pit closures that followed nearly a decade after the Miners Strike of 1984–85. At the start of the programme, Brenda did not support the strike and was worried about its negative effects on her husband and children. The programme follows her change of heart and her growing involvement with the campaign. At the end, Brenda stands on a picket line alongside her husband and other miners' wives. Like *Framed Youth*, the programme showed budding activists what was possible, while at the same time drawing attention to the scarcity of opportunities for them to be seen and heard on television on their own terms.

The same year he saw 'Major, the Miners and Me', O'Connor was on his way to Greece to plant trees as part of an environmental campaign. Stopping off to visit friends in London he heard about plans for the M11 link road, then in the early stages of construction, which would mean the uprooting of 1000 trees and the demolition of over 250 houses along its route. There were daily actions to try and slow the building of the road, which was displacing communities and threatening local wildlife. Within days of his arrival in London, after squatting some of the houses set for demolition,

Opposite: Contents of *POUT Issue 1*, from VHS sleeve (POUT, 1992).

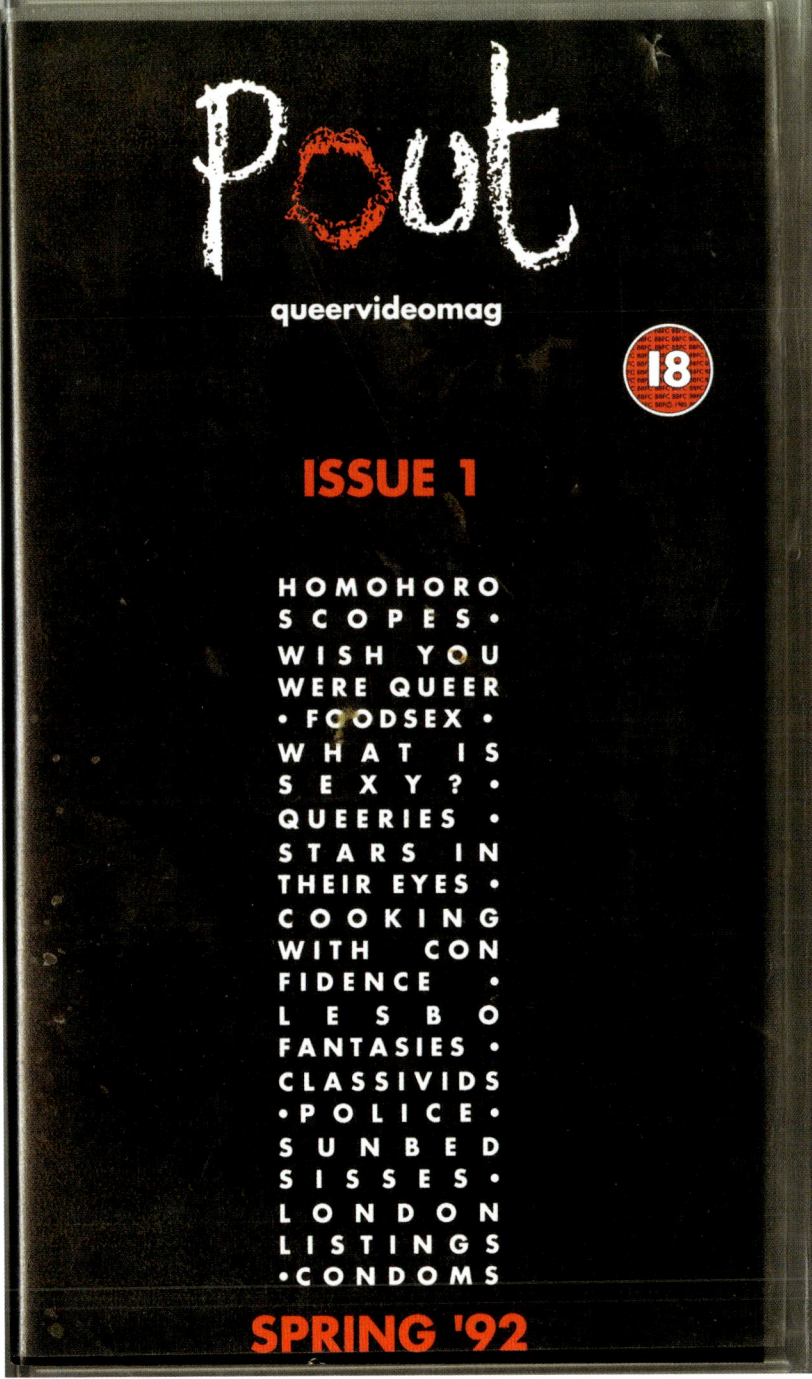

POUT Issue 1 (POUT, 1992).

O'Connor set up home in a 250-year-old sweet chestnut tree in Wanstead, East London, that was scheduled for removal.

O'Connor soon swapped the stills camera he had been using to document the action for a video camera and decided to focus his attention on trees closer to home. The clashes between the campaigners, the police and the security firms hired to put a stop to the occupation were largely hidden from public view, as they took place behind large wooden hoardings. O'Connor contacted the producers of *Video Diaries,* hoping to borrow a video camera to record his experiences as an environmental campaigner. At first, the producers were unsure, but O'Connor persuaded them that he could get them footage of protests against the Criminal Justice Bill, and they eventually loaned him a small camcorder. O'Connor quickly realised that the video camera would serve multiple purposes, just as it had in earlier activist video projects: it could record the violent behaviour of security guards and the police; it could be used as evidence in court to support the cases of the campaigners; and it could help to publicise the campaign: in the evenings, at a community centre opposite the occupied tree, the protestors started to show compilations of the footage of the action taking place behind the hoardings. The producers of *Video Diaries* never saw that camera again, and O'Connor didn't get his video shown on the BBC, but these screening events provided opportunities for the local community to find out what was going on behind the hoardings in their neighbourhood and encouraged them to get involved in the campaign.

Through Zoe Broughton, a comrade from the M11 campaign, O'Connor was introduced to Thomas Harding and Jamie Hartzell, who had become disillusioned with the 'bureaucracy and political claustrophobia'[9] they had experienced producing television programmes for broadcast, and with the way environmental issues were being covered unfairly – if at all – by mainstream media. When O'Connor first met them, the pair had just had some success using their previous media experience to help a group of villagers in

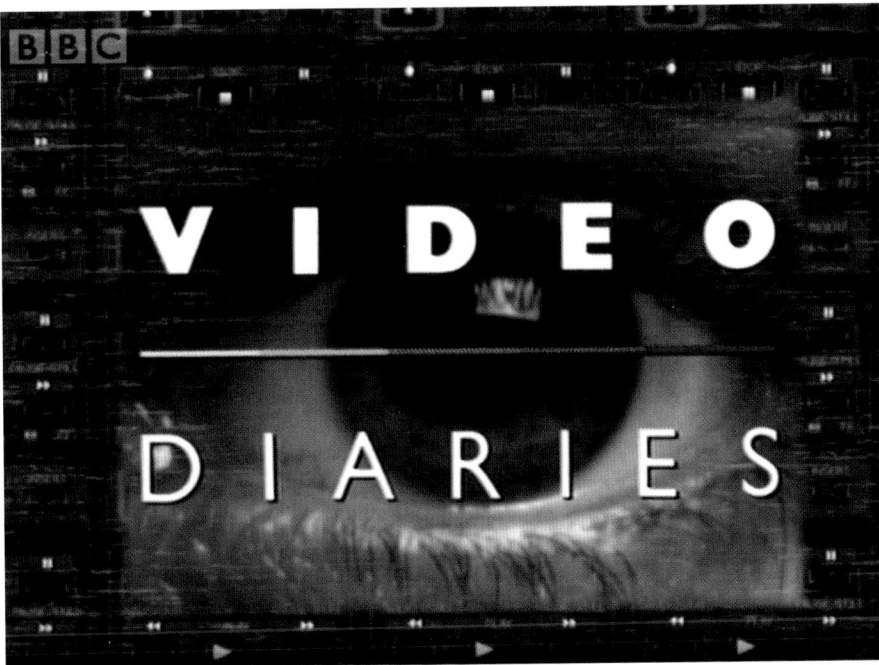

Video Diaries (BBC, 1990).

Paul O'Connor videoing Reclaim the Streets, 1997.

Hampshire who were trying to stop a golf course from being built on nearby common land. Ultimately the golf club was prosecuted by the animal welfare charity the Royal Society for the Prevention of Cruelty to Animals (RSPCA) with the help of video evidence collected by Harding and Hartzell that showed the developers actively killing endangered wildlife.

Initially, there were five people separately making videos of the M11 road protests and occupations, and they wanted to consolidate what they had been recording to share it further afield to raise awareness and build support for the campaign. Following an initial meeting with Harding and Hartzell, the group collectivised under the name Small World Media, setting up their own edit suite and beginning to sift through over 100 hours of video collected from various environmental grassroots campaigns. In April 1994, the first edition of their new alternative news video magazine, undercurrents, was ready to share. Ninety minutes long, it offered 'a roundup of stories that television ignores, marginalises or fails to cover,'[10] including features on the Criminal Justice Bill and a report titled 'You've Got to be Choking', documenting the campaign to stop the M11 Link road in East London. Small World produced an initial run of 250 copies and sent out 10,000 flyers in the hopes that they would get noticed. Borrowing from the community screenings that had been organised opposite the tree, they held a screening event for 100 people in a squatted church in North London. The tape was soon reviewed in *Time Out* magazine, which described it as 'The Pathe News of the 90s.'[11] The *Independent* and the *Guardian* newspapers also wrote about it and included the group's phone number, which resulted in a second production run and the sale of over 500 copies in the first month. Following a feature on Carlton Television's *The Little Picture Show* (ITV, 1993–95), a cultural magazine series devoted to video, the group was inundated with orders. In the spirit of integrated production and distribution, the group took the video on tour, showing and selling it at festivals not just in the UK but also all over Europe, finally selling over 1,000 copies of the first issue.

Between 1994 and 1999, undercurrents produced ten issues of the video magazine. Each tape included documentation of actions directed largely

Campaigner Patsy Braga protesting the demolition of her home to make way for the M11 link road (*undercurrents No. 1*, 1994).

undercurrents No. 1 (undercurrents, 1994).

at environmental concerns and miscarriages of justice. This was intercut with footage collected from international campaigns against the agents of global capitalism, including banks, large corporations and fossil fuel companies. The themes and aesthetics of the items included on each issue were broadly similar, but their focus and reach extended from the national to the global. The video magazine enabled all of these different actions to inhabit the same space; by creating such a polyphonic compilation, undercurrents served to express the size and power of the movement, making its protests harder to dismiss as isolated events.

Like its predecessors, undercurrents continued to use video as a mode of witness and to create campaign videos. What was different about this later stage of video activism was the increasing awareness on both sides of the viewfinder: growing familiarity with the technology meant activists could be more critical of the ability of video to achieve their aims, while those in power grew more confident about how they could turn the cameras back on the activists. Thomas Harding's *The Video Activist Handbook*, first published in 2001, describes three different functions of 'witness video' being produced at the time: first, as 'a pacifier to calm things down in situations of conflict'; second, as 'defence against false arrest or violent assault at demonstrations'; and finally, as 'offence when gathering evidence of some illegal or immoral activity.'[12] All three functions can be found in earlier video activist projects.

Harding acknowledges that the presence of video cameras would sometimes elicit heightened, often boisterous 'performances' from activists. This kind of behaviour led some video activists to wonder whether video evidence might cause problems for those involved if it fell into the wrong hands and showed them being disorderly or carrying out apparently criminal behaviour. At the same time, there was a growing recognition of the political value of media spectacle, and activists were able to harness the specific power of the video camera while carrying out potentially unlawful actions to draw attention to injustice and create dramatic scenes. This could subsequently be used to highlight the creeping criminalisation of specific acts of protest and dissent. On the other side, authorities had become fearful and suspicious of these same video cameras, resulting in some video-makers being singled out and refused entry to or removed from protests. Many of the undercurrents tapes during this period are punctuated by shots of angry police officers and private security guards snatching away video cameras, pushing them to the ground or demanding they be switched off. The willingness of broadcasters to air footage recorded by non-union members on cheap camcorders meant that large audiences could get a grassroots perspective of an action that might otherwise be ignored or misrepresented. However, selling footage to television outlets became a contentious issue for some video activists, who feared that such footage could be used to sensationalise, incriminate or misrepresent a particular action.

By the mid-1990s, with increased use of video surveillance on both sides, some activists were so wary of being caught on camera and convicted that there were many instances of abuse and aggression towards anyone holding a video camera. Other campaigners, meanwhile, were experiencing video fatigue. It often felt like there were more people with video cameras

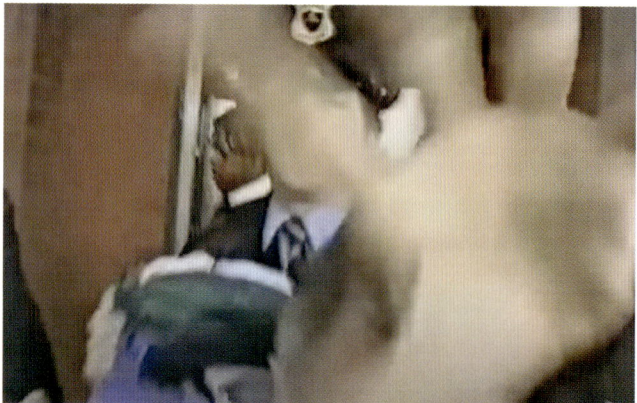

Images from *undercurrents* (1994-99).

than activists; hours of footage were being recorded with no sense of what or whom it was for, or where it might be screened. To mitigate against this, undercurrents argued for a clearly and collectively defined purpose and distribution strategy before deploying a video camera; they also proposed a practice of asking for consent before videoing someone. These are concerns that continue to resonate in the present.

The tenth and final issue of undercurrents' video magazine was produced in 1999 and included information about a planned day of protest, action and carnival in financial centres across the globe; an update of environmental, social and animal justice direct actions around Britain at the time; documentation of one woman's journey delivering aid to war-torn Kosovo; and a report of an Oxford community fighting back when transport authority Railtrack ignored residents' views and destroyed the Greenbelt. The issue differs from earlier ones, using fast-cut editing techniques, text on screen and graphics, mimicking the aesthetics of television youth programming at the time. It also includes several satirical takedowns of 'top capitalists', councils and government agencies, as well as a number of musical interludes, including a 'musical tribute to the daft policing of protests!' and a comedic music video highlighting the New Labour government's arms sales to repressive regimes.

The completion of the final VHS edition coincided with undercurrents' first attempt at video streaming. undercurrents had been using a rudimentary email service called Pegasus since 1993, and by 1997 they had their first website; both were used to promote the sale of videos, explain who they were and stay in touch with their growing audience and network of contributors. For many video activists at this time, broadcasting anything over 30 seconds on the web still felt like a pipe dream.[13] A year after O'Connor's limited success live streaming footage collected at the 'J18' Carnival against Capitalism protests, he travelled to Washington, using email to help co-ordinate large groups of activists who were covering mobilisations against the International Monetary Fund and the World Bank. This project took place under the wider umbrella of Indymedia, 'a network of individuals, independent and alternative media activists and organisations, offering grassroots, non-corporate, non-commercial coverage of important social and political issues.'[14] Collectively, these groups were able to support anyone with internet access to upload text, still images or short audio or video files directly to a centralised reporting website.

With the actions spanning several days, people could now directly communicate with one another around the globe and upload recordings representing their own experiences of the demonstration:

> While many corporate news networks were reporting the restraint of the police, visitors to the Washington Indymedia site could both see the images and hear the sounds of peaceful men and women being beaten, tear-gassed, and viciously attacked with pepper spray.[15]

Indymedia UK further developed this use of the Internet to create what they termed 'Direct Media' to cover the Mayday 2000 actions in London. As their mission statement from the time explained,

> Through this system of 'Direct Media', Indymedia erodes the dividing line between reporters and reported, between active producers and passive audience: people are enabled to speak for themselves. Direct media = media as party, education, direct action, entertainment, empowerment.[16]

'Public Access Terminals' were set up on the streets alongside the activists, allowing anyone present to immediately and directly broadcast their experiences over the web. Following this mass co-ordinated action and subsequent transmission, Indymedia's London contingent established its own open publishing site as part of the wider global Indymedia network. Through this network and website they were able to report on other actions and make visible some of the events and issues which were routinely misrepresented or suppressed by mainstream media channels. As a continuation of the work of undercurrents and a precursor to the connected and networked spread of video activism that would follow in the 2010s, Indymedia UK had, by 2003, developed a decentralised approach similar to that of the 1980s workshops, setting up a network of centres around the country under the name IMC United Kollektives.

The work of POUT, OUTRAGE! and undercurrents was made possible by the availability of cheaper and more sophisticated video equipment, and reflects the ongoing failure of mainstream media to fairly cover social and environmental justice movements in the UK. The three groups signalled a new wave of video activism, characterised by a single-issue focus, networked

undercurrents No. 10 (undercurrents, 1999).

campaigning and a growing awareness of the power of creating media spectacles – such as smaller but more frequent group actions, occupations and banner drops – in place of one-off large rallies and marches.

Reflecting in 2020 on the journey from that time to today's smartphone era, Paul O'Connor concluded that the capacity to instantly upload and stream video has been a mixed blessing for video activists: 'we gained global and immediate distribution, but with too many images, I believe, we have lost effectiveness.'[17] For O'Connor, and many others, live-streaming video straight from mobile phones entailed risks of footage of protests and actions being copied and shared by third parties for malicious purposes, perhaps to incriminate a group or individual or to misrepresent a specific case. O'Connor, however, remains optimistic about the use of video cameras to support specific, often local activist campaigns, as long as activists remember what was key to the work of undercurrents:

> We must remain strategic: before making a video to be shared to further the cause of any kind of activism, we must always ask why we are a producing a video, who we are aiming it at and what do we want to achieve by doing it.[18]

Close-up: AIDS Activist Video

The creators of POUT and members of OUTRAGE! drew on art and activism to get their messages heard and seen. This recalled the early days of video activism, when the distinction between video art and activist video was less defined.[19] Many artists identified as activists and vice versa; both shared an understanding of experimentation and were eager to use new technology to support urgent political work. In the 1970s, this could be seen in new experimental feminist video projects. By the 1980s, artists were using video to explore representations of race, as well as to draw attention to the experiences of people living with AIDS.

The first AIDS activist video in the UK was made in 1983 by Stuart Marshall, who was a deeply involved with British video art as a practitioner, curator and theorist, co-founding London Video Arts in 1976 to further the promotion, distribution and exhibition of video art. Marshall's *Kaposi's Sarcoma: A Plague and its Symptoms* (1983) explores how AIDS was represented by the dominant media, in particular medical journalism, and how this portrayal worked to 'destroy the work of gay liberation that had come before, transforming the homoerotic body into a pathologised and morbid body.'[20] As a result, the urgent work of creating alternative images from within the community of those most impacted by HIV/AIDS was concerned as much with developing modes of self-representation as with survival, education and campaigning.

The different modes of UK AIDS activist videos in the 1980s and early 90s mirror the wider story of video activism, in which form was not fixed, but dictated by content and context. Examples ranged from issue-oriented educational videos, among them safer sex tapes such as artist Sunil Gupta's *Cock Crazy or Scared Stiff* (1992); documentation of civil disobedience, notably in the work of OUTRAGE!; sympathetic and honest portraits of people affected by HIV/AIDS, such as Isaac Julien's *This is Not an AIDS Advertisement* or Phillip Timmins' *Compromised Immunity* (both 1987), an adaptation of a stage play about the relationship between a heterosexual nurse and a gay patient who has AIDS; and finally, videos critiquing or presenting a corrective to mainstream media representations of AIDS, for example *A Plague on You: AIDS, the Media and the Truth* (Lesbian and Gay Media Group, 1985), shown in the BBC's *Open Space* (1983–95) slot.

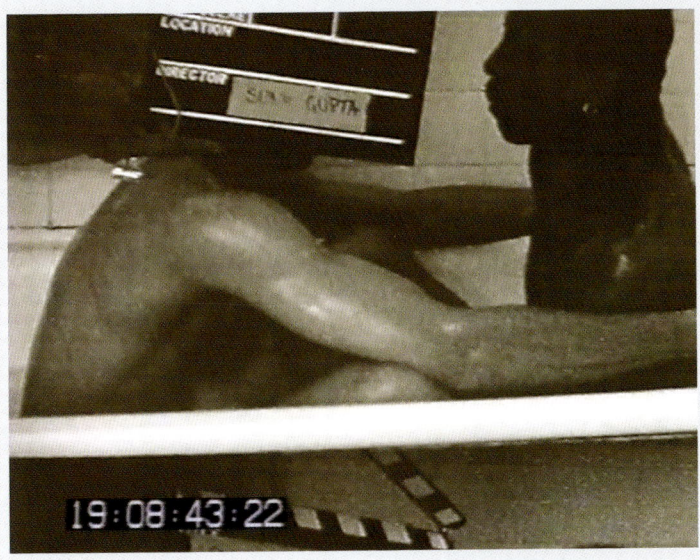

Cock Crazy or Scared Stiff (Sunil Gupta, 1992).

Marshall drew on his experience organising informal screenings of artist videos in non-traditional screening spaces to find similarly receptive audiences for his videos in gay clubs. This type of screening opportunity interested him much more than television because it allowed him to 'speak to a very specific group about a specific set of interests',[21] free of editorial restrictions: 'to make a piece for broadcast television is always in some sense to go along with the ideology of the broadcasters.'[22]

Even so, Marshall would later make two programmes about HIV/AIDS for Channel 4: *Bright Eyes* (1984) and *Over Our Dead Bodies* (1991), demonstrating how alternative AIDS media production could, at the same time, be both cynical *and* optimistic about the power of broadcast media. The same could be said of later AIDS activist videos produced for television, such as Pratibha Parmar's *Reframing AIDS* (Channel Four, 1987), or adopting television modes, like the magazine-style video *Mouthing Off: Women Speak Out about Safer Sex* (Leeds AIDS Advice Group, 1991).

It's clear that while many AIDS activist tapes appropriated mass media techniques and platforms to convey their message, what distinguished them from their broadcast counterparts was the means of production or distribution, which always originated from within and catered for the community of those impacted by HIV/AIDS.

EPILOGUE: VIDEO ACTIVISM 2.0

With the arrival of the internet, it might seem that the dream of 1970s video activism had come true. Certainly, it has never been easier to make and share activist videos. Web 2.0 and the rise of social media brought with them the promise of global and instant connectivity and open-access broadcasting, seemingly beyond the control of traditional mainstream media. But over time, traditional media has colonised the online space, while social media platforms have begun to replace or be co-opted by the very channels that activists seek to subvert and challenge. Far from remaining a neutral space, the World Wide Web has become dominated by commerce and vast social media empires, which have become unimaginably rich on the proceeds of advertising and the mining of users' data.

Activists have grown wary of content overload and the narrowing effects of algorithms, with the very real 'echo chambers' many users have begun to experience as proof of this. At the same time, users have less agency and autonomy; content and accounts can be suppressed, blocked, suspended or terminated, instantly and with little or no accountability, by risk averse or increasingly politically assertive host platforms.

Loose, often temporary networks with common interests or focuses are able to use hashtags to spread their message quickly and collectively through spontaneously-produced videos. The form of these videos often mimics what has proven popular in other online videos. They tend to be, at most, a few minutes long, comprised of fast edits and short takes. Often, they rely on satire and aspire to become a meme; at other times, they take the form of sincere and urgent unedited direct addresses to camera, created and uploaded by individuals. Adding a further layer of complexity, the same means of representation activists use to challenge the oppression of marginalised groups and under-represented experiences have been adopted and adapted by the far right and by political opportunists with oppositional aims and dangerous results.

Much as email did in the early 2000s, social media activism and the sharing of videos helps to mobilise protesters and sustain feelings of collective action, fostering interaction and participation at a global scale. Smaller activist media groups, with a focus on specific, local topics, continue to use video as one of a number of media strategies to raise awareness around specific campaigns or issues. This current period of video activism is still very much in its infancy, but we need only look to the uprisings in Iran in 2009 and the Black Lives Matter and #MeToo movements of the 2010s to see the integral role of online video in building mass movements, documenting state violence and providing a platform to demand change. This approach has been effectively used to directly address and challenge perpetrators, to highlight injustices and, often, to shame those in power into enacting change.

In 2022, Kwajo Tweneboa became a voice for social housing tenants in the UK, holding landlords to account using Instagram to share videos documenting poorly managed and maintained council accommodation and housing association properties, naming and shaming landlords and forcing housing providers to respond. These videos are strongly reminiscent in their intention and aesthetic to the damp tapes made 50 years earlier. We have also seen environmental activists Extinction Rebellion and Just Stop Oil make and share videos of their eye-catching actions and campaigns, mirroring the theatrics and intentions documented and shared by undercurrents in their video magazines from the 1990s.

Since the 1970s, the social and technological landscape in the UK has engendered new modes of activism, powered by increased access to ever more portable, affordable and connected video technology. But for all the many benefits that can be ascribed to these new forms of representation, there are criticisms, too; as Raymond Williams presciently observed in 1975, the development and application of all technological devices – from the Portapak to Instagram – are determined by and reflective of the social relations out of which they are produced.¹ Forty years later, contemporary theorist Hannah Black noted that the internet had 'come to look more like the non-Internet world: structured by the demands of profit, violent, strange, funny, awful, beautiful, full of desire and the alienation of desire ... everything that the world is.'²

There is a growing suspicion and cynicism surrounding the internet, particularly among those who remain excluded from the wider conversation and have seen little benefit in the form of structural change. Government-sanctioned austerity has resulted in increased privatisation and control of public spaces, making collective organising in person and in public harder than ever, while activity online is monitored by the state for criminal activity, or by vast corporations for profit. Alarmist rhetoric characterises much protest and activism as 'extremism', and for every claim or argument made on video there appears to be a counter video. Debates around 'cancel culture' and the power of platforming or not platforming certain positions are evidence of the necessity for nuance, caution and care when engaging with new technologies.

At the same time, early critiques of activist video practices persist. These include the risks of 'othering' participants with the patronising assumptions that accompany a 'saviour discourse' of 'reanimating' and 'empowering' specific groups or individuals who are presumed to be otherwise inanimate and disempowered, alongside the very real fears of being surveilled and incriminated by footage often recorded in good faith. All of this raises important questions around who has power and access, and how material is produced and shared.

With each new development in the story of video activism, the participants and producers of activist video projects have grown more familiar and fluent with the potential of media representation, and more conscious of its limits. This greater understanding has made possible new approaches to production, distribution and exhibition that take account of criticisms of previous methods, and that remain contingent on both the subject matter of the video and the context in which it is being made. Activist video practices continue to provide a means for individuals and groups to use a video camera to look at the world in which they live, and to share their findings and experiences on their own terms.

The specific collective process of planning, recording, editing and sharing an activist video continues to provide time and space to find commonalities and explore differences. Activists involved in the production of these videos are part of an act of making that affords an increased awareness of and reflection on their lived experience. And this, in turn, helps to build resilience, foster solidarity and create change.

FURTHER READING

Roy Armes, *On Video* (Routledge, 1988)
Ron Bailey, *The Squatters* (Penguin Books, 1973)
Houston A. Baker, Manthia Diawara and Ruth H. Lindeborg, *Black British Cultural Studies: A Reader* (Chicago: University of Chicago Press, 1996)
Petra Bauer and Dan Kidner, *Working Together: Notes on British Film Collectives in the 1970s* (Focal Point Gallery, 2013)
Simon Biggs, 'Using Video as a Therapeutic Tool', in *Journal of Centre of Advanced TV Studies*, vol 8, 1980
Andi Biren and Audrey Bronstein, *Basic Video in Community Work* (Inter-Action Imprint, 1975)
Ina Blom, *The Autobiography of Video* (Sternberg Press, 2016)
Paul Bonner, 'Broadcast Access Television and Its Future Development' (BBC, 1976)
Deirdre Boyle, *Subject to Change: Guerrilla Television Revisited* (Oxford University Press, 1997)
Su Braden, *Artists and People* (Routledge & Kegan Paul, 1978)
Paul de Bruyne and Pascal Gielen, *Community Art the Politics of Trespassing* (Valiz, 2013)
Sue Clayton, and Laura Mulvey, *Other Cinemas: Politics, Culture and Experimental Film in the 1970s* (I.B. Tauris, 2017)
Rosalind Coward, *Liberation Films Distribution Catalogue* (Liberation Films, 1978)
Margaret Dickinson, *Rogue Reels: Oppositional Film Making in Britain, 1945–90* (BFI, 1999)
Tony Dowmunt, et al, *Inclusion through Media* (Mute Publishing, 2007)
Tony Dowmunt, *Video with Young People* (Inter-Action, 1980)
Brian Groombridge, *Television and the People a Programme for Democratic* (Penguin Books, 1972)
Roger Hallas, *Participation Reframing Bodies: AIDS, Bearing Witness, and the Queer Moving Image* (Duke University Press, 2009)
Thomas Harding, *The Video Activist Handbook* (London: Pluto Press, 2001)
Robert Hewison, and John Holden, *Experience and Experiment: the UK Branch of the Calouste Gulbenkian Foundation, 1956–2006* (Calouste Gulbenkian Foundation, UK Branch, 2006)
Bert Hogenkamp, *Deadly Parallels: Film and the Left in Britain, 1929–1939* (Dagenham: Lawrence and Wishart, 2000)

John Hopkins et al, *Video in Community Development* (Ovum 1972)

Alexandra Juhasz, 'No Woman Is an Object: Realizing the Feminist Collaborative Video' in *Camera Obscura* vol. 18 no. 3, December 2003, pp.71–97.

Alexandra Juhasz, *AIDS TV: Identity, Community, and Alternative Video* (Duke University Press, 1995)

Owen Kelly, *Community, Art and the State: Storming the Citadels* (Comedia / Marion Boyars, 1984)

Frances Kerrigan, *Theories and Practices of Video Work* (Middlesex Polytechnic Media Research Group, 1975)

Julia Knight, *Diverse Practices: A Critical Reader on British Video Art* (University of Luton Press, 1996)

Charles Landry, *What a Way to Run a Railroad: An Analysis of Radical Failure* (Comedia, 1985)

Nick Lunch and Chris Lunch, *Insights into Participatory Video: A Handbook for the Field* (Insight, 2006)

Paolo Magagnoli, *Documents of Utopia the Politics of Experimental Documentary* (Columbia University Press, 2015)

Sarita Malik et al, *Community Filmmaking: Diversity, Practices and Places* (Taylor & Francis, 2017)

Janine Marchessault, *Mirror Machine: Video and Identity* (YYZ Books, 1995)

James McInnes, *Video in Education and Training* (Focal Press, 1980)

Marshall McLuhan, *Understanding Media: the Extensions of Man* (Abacus, 1974)

Kobena Mercer, *Welcome to the Jungle: New Positions in Black Cultural Studies* (London: Routledge, 1994)

Heinz Nigg and Graham Wade, *Community Media: Community Communication in the UK: Video, Local TV, Film and Photography* (Regenbogen-Verl, 1980)

Heinz Nigg, *Rebel Video: The Video Movement of the 1970s and 1980s: London, Bern, Lausanne, Basel, Zurich* (Scheidegger & Spiess, 2017)

Jan O'Malley, *The Politics of Community Action. A Decade of Struggle in Notting Hill* (Spokesman, 1977)

Jackie Shaw and Clive Robertson, *Participatory Video: a Practical Guide to Using Video Creatively in Group Development Work* (Routledge, 1997)

Yvonne Spielmann, *Video: The Reflexive Medium* (MIT Press, 2008)

Graham Wade, *Street Video* (Blackthorn Press, 1980)

John A Walker, *Left Shift: Radical Art in 1970s Britain* (I.B. Tauris, 2002)

Thomas Waugh et al, *Challenge for Change: Activist Documentary at the National Film Board of Canada* (MQUP, 2014)

Chris Weedon, *Identity and Culture: Narratives of Difference and Belonging* (London / Maidenhead: Open University Press, 2009)

Thomas Waugh, *'Show Us Life': Toward a History and Aesthetics of the Committed Documentary* (Scarecrow, 1984)

White, Shirley A *Participatory Video: Images That Transform and Empower* (Sage Publications, 2003)

Alfred Willener et al, *Videology and Utopia: Explorations in a New Medium* (Routledge / Taylor & Francis Group, 2016)

PLAYLIST

*Video can be found at **www.the-lcva.co.uk**

Handsworth Songs (John Akomfrah / Black Audio Film Collective, 1986)
August 13th: What Happened? (Albany Video, 1977)*
March to Aldermaston (1959)
Please Adjust Your Eyes (Basement News / Hackney Gorillas)*
Into the Darkness (Tony Dowmunt / WACAT, 1977)*
Felix Dennis on The Frost Programme (ITV, tx. 7/11/1970) youtube.com/watch?v=WxjnfDToQmA accessed 20/04/2024
Sweet 16 (Carry Gorney (Inter-Action / Channel 40, 1977)*
Things That Mother Never Told Us! (Carry Gorney, Inter-Action/Channel 40, 1979)*
Forming a Resident's Association (Graft On!, 1974)
Song of Long Ago (Graft On!, 1975)*
How to Use a Portapack (Sue Hall & John Hopkins, 1978)*
Squat Now While Stocks Last (Sue Hall & John Hopkins, 1974)*
The Amazing Story of Talacre (InFilms, 1971)*
Inter-Action Media Van (Inter-Action, 1974)*
Who Killed Colin Roach? (Isaac Julien / Sankofa, 1983)*
Step Forward Youth (Dave Kinoshi / Menelik Shabazz, 1977)*
Frostbite (John Kirk, 1970) vimeo.com/87537287 accessed 20 April 2024
VTR St-Jacques (Bonnie Klein, National Film Board of Canada, 1969)
All You Need's an Excuse (Liberation Films, 1972)*
End of a Tactic (Liberation Films, 1969)*
Fly a Flag for Poplar (Liberation Films, 1974)*
Starting to Happen (Liberation Films, 1974)*

PLAYLIST

A Woman's Place (Liberation Films, 1971)*
Fight the Cuts (Oval Video, 1979)
Open Door: East End Channel 1 (Maggie Pinhorn, 1973)*
E1 Festival (Tower Hamlets Arts Project, 1974)*
Do You Love Me? (TVX, 1970)
Video Space (TVX, 1970)
Community Video 1980 (Joel Venet (Liberation Films, 1980)*
The Battle for Powis Square (West London Media Workshop, 1974)*
Murcheson Tenants (West London Media Workshop (c. 1977)*
News at West 10 (West London Media Workshop, 1976–77)
Black Homelessness (West London Media Workshop, 1978)*
Pepys Estate – Organising (John White / Geoff Stow, 1974)*
Pepys Estate Repairs Campaign (John White / Geoff Stow, 1974)*
The Hard Stop (George Amponsah, 2015)
True Romance (Big Flame/Newsreel Collective 1982)
Framed Youth: Revenge of the Teenage Perverts (London Lesbian and Gay Youth Video Project, 1983)*
OUTRAGE! Tapes (Mark Harriott, 1994)*
The People's Account (Ceddo Film and Video Workshop, 1985)*
POUT Video Magazine, Issues 1–3 (POUT, 1994)*
Step Forward Youth (Menelik Shabazz, 1977)*
undercurrents Alternative News Video, Issues 1–10 (undercurrents, 1994)*
Miners' Campaign Tapes (Platform Films, 1984)

NOTES

INTRODUCTION

1. John Hopkins, Cliff Evans, Steve Herman & John Kirk (1972/3), *Video in Community Development* (University of Southampton/Centre for Advanced Television Studies).
2. See Bert Hogenkamp (1983), *Deadly Parallels: Film and the Left in Britain, 1929–39.* (London: Lawrence and Wishart Ltd.)
3. This book would not have been possible without The London Community Video Archive, which was established in 2016 to preserve, archive and share community videos made in the 1970s/80s in London and the South East. www.the-lcva.co.uk.
4. Tony Dowmunt (2009), 'A Whited Sepulchre, Autobiography and Video Diaries in "Post Documentary" Culture', PhD Thesis (London: Goldsmiths University), p. 123.

CHAPTER 1

1. Kenneth Tynan (2013), 'Observer Archive, 1968: The Arts Lab, a Ramshackle Prototype for the ICA'. *The Guardian* (27 Apr.). Available at www.theguardian.com/news/2013/apr/28/arts-laboratory-kenneth-tynan-archive (accessed 26 Feb. 2024).
2. Bradley Martin, 'International Times Archive. http://www.internationaltimes.it/archive/index.php?year=1967&volume=IT-Volume-1&issue=12 (accessed. 6 Nov. 2014).
3. 'The Development of Community Arts with the Arts Council' (1974) (London: V&A Archives) (accessed March 2015).
4. Following the closure of the Arts Lab in 1969, Moore moved to Amsterdam, where he helped to create a similar venture to the Arts Lab, the Melkweg (the Milky Way), and continued to be involved with video for the rest of his life. Haynes moved to Paris, where he taught Media Studies and Sexual Politics for 30 years at the University of Paris.

5. Heinz Nigg and Andy Porter. 'John 'Hoppy' Hopkins'. *ww.the-lcva.co.uk*, 2017, www.the-lcva.co.uk/interviews/58db835cf6aab40c5cfa3748.
6. Jackie Hatfield, 'Artists' Video in the 70's & 80's: [sic] Interview with Sue Hall & John Hopkins'. 17 Nov. 2004. *Rewind*, uodwebservices.co.uk/documents/Sue%20Hall,%20John%20Hopkins/SHJH506.pdf (accessed 9 Sept. 2019).
7. Ibid.
8. 'Lumps and Grumps'. *Time Out*, 1969, [issue unknown], p. 29.
9. Ibid.
10. Transcript of Interview with Sue Hall & John Hopkins: London, 7 Feb. 2005. Interview by Chris Meigh Andrews. http://www.meigh-andrews.com/writings/interviews/sue-hall-john-hopkins (accessed 6 Nov. 2014).
11. Ibid.
12. Transcript of Interview with John Hopkins by Heinz Nigg and Andy Porter, UK, 2015, www.the-lcva.co.uk (accessed August 2017).
13. Ibid.
14. Ibid.
15. Ibid.
16. Footage of the invasion from the BBC can be found from John Kirk at www.vimeo.com/87537287
17. 'Video – the Frost Hijack', in *Friends*, London, 11 Dec. 1970 (20th ed.), p. 10.
18. Transcript of Interview with John 'Hoppy' Hopkins by Heinz Nigg and Andy Porter.
19. John Hopkins et al., *Video in Community Development*, (London: Ovum, 1973).
20. Launched in 1970 in New York, *Radical Software* was the first publication dedicated to the exploration of the application of low-gauge video technology.
21. 'Sony Annual Report', Sony Group Corporation, 1970, p. 6.

CHAPTER 2

1. Andy Porter, unpublished interview with the author, July 2017.
2. Published in *Community Media: Community Communication in the UK: Video, Local TV, Film, and Photography* (Nigg and Wade, Zürich: Regenbogen-Verlag, 1980), is a research report compiled from pamphlets, articles, grant applications and interviews with community media practtioners working in the 1970s. The chapter on West London Media Workshop provides an in-depth case study of the group's development over a three-year period.
3. Ibid., p. 64.

4. Ibid.
5. Paul Bonner, 'Broadcast access television and its future development,' British Broadcasting Corporation mimeo (London: BBC, 1976), pp. 1–2.
6. David Attenborough (1972), 'Community Programmes', in BBC Written Archives, Centre R78/2/540/1 Access Programmes.
7. Giles Oakley, 'Opening Up the Box', in Janet Willis & Tana Wollen (eds.), *The Broadcasting Debate No. 5: The Neglected Audience* (London: British Film Institute, 1990), p. 16.
8. Ibid., p. 18.
9. Fred Johnson, 'Vox Pops – The BBC's Community Programme Unit' in *The Independent* (Cambridge, MA], June 1990, pp. 30–4.
10. *Open Door* was renamed *Open Space* in 1983. In the 1990s, with the availability of new handheld, domestic camcorders, the BBC's Community Programme Unit launched a new initiative, *Video Nation* (BBC2, 1994–98). Between 1993 and 2001, the BBC provided camcorders and basic training to a selection of 50 people to record aspects of their everyday lives. One of these participants was Paul O'Connor, who used his camcorder to document direct action road protests and the UK's thriving counterculture. Following his work and training with a camcorder, O'Connor went on to co-found Undercurrents, an independent production and distribution alternative news agency for videos produced by grassroots environmental and social justice campaigners.
11. Peter Lewis, *Mercenaries and Missionaries – a Marriage of Convenience: A Personal Account of Bristol Channel and Community Media*, https://ravenrow.org/texts/peter-lewis-mercenaries-and-missionaries-a-marriage-of-convenience-a-personal-account-of-bristol-channel-and-community-media#footnotes (accessed 7 Aug. 2025)
12. Fred Johnson, 'Vox Pops – The BBC's Community Programme Unit', pp. 30–4.
13. Heinz Nigg and Graham Wade, *Community Media: Community Communication in the UK: Video, Local TV, Film, and Photography* (Zurich: Regenbogen-Verl, 1980), pp. 100–1.
14. Ibid.
15. Ibid., p. 27.
16. Ibid., p. 28.
17. Interview with Carry Gorney, https://the-lcva.co.uk/interviews/59a682b81de57817c5ce5ac2 (accessed Sept. 2017).
18. Carry Gorney, interview with the author, 2 May 2012.
19. Su Braden, *Artists and People* (London: Routledge and Kegan Paul, 1978) p. 151.

20. Peter Lewis, *Mercenaries and Missionaries*.
21. *Video Active Report*, 1985.
22. Tower Hamlets Arts Project (THAP) was previously home to The Basement Project.
23. https://vimeo.com/ondemand/despitetv/372852428 (accessed 7 Aug. 2025).
24. *Video Active Report*, 1985.
25. It wouldn't be until the early 1980s, with the launch of Channel 4 and the Workshop Declaration that broadcast television saw the structural changes that would again grant some minority groups access to the airwaves (See Chapter 5).
26. Heinz Nigg and Graham Wade, *Community Media: Community Communication in the UK: Video, Local TV, Film, and Photography* (Zurich: Regenbogen-Verlag, 1980), p. 186.
27. Ibid., p. 24.
28. John Buston, *The Report of the Community Arts Working Party* (London: Arts Council of Great Britain, 1974), p. 3.
29. Owen Kelly, *Community, Art, and the State: Storming the Citadels* (London: Comedia Pub. Group in Association with Marion Boyars, 1984), p. 17

CHAPTER 3

1. 'The Aylesbury Estate, the Latest Front in the Battle against Social Cleansing', www.redpepper.org.uk/the-aylesbury-estate-the-latest-front-in-the-battle-against-social-cleansing (accessed 28 Feb. 2024).
2. Watchful Eye, 'Watchful Eye' vimeo.com/watchfuleye (accessed 28 Feb. 2024).
3. Jan O'Malley, *The Politics of Community Action. A Decade of Struggle in Notting Hill* (Spokesman, 1977) p. 100.
4. 'Film Tape Allowed in Court', *The Guardian* [London], 23 August 1974.
5. Heinz Nigg and Andy Porter, interview with John 'Hoppy' Hopkins, 2014.
6. The relationship between TV broadcasters and the work of self-organised community video practitioners at the time was fraught. The trade union ACTT opposed the broadcasting of footage not recorded by their members. Hopkins describes them as 'gate-keepers to what material was allowed to be broadcast, and only in exceptional circumstances did they allow this to happen ….' The studio circumvented the limits set by the union by using a television camera to record from the video playback monitor. They were then able to broadcast the footage of the eviction, bypassing the need to feed the material through the television system. (Chris Meigh Andrews, 'Transcript of Interview with Sue Hall & John Hopkins, London, 7 Feb. 2005'. https://www.meigh-andrews.com/writings/interviews/sue-hall-john-hopkins. (accessed 28 Feb. 2024).

7. 'People's Tube', *Time Out*, year and date unknown (article appears in exhibition catalogue for *The Video Show*, The Serpentine Gallery, 1975)
8. Sue Hall and John Hopkins, 'Socio-Cultural Applications of Television Technology in the UK'. London: Council for Cultural Co-operation, 1975, p. 18 (accessed at Central St Martins Study Collection, London, February, 2015).
9. Heinz Nigg and Andy Porter, transcript of Interview with Sue Hall.
10. Interview with Sue Hall by Ed Webb-Ingall, London, July, 2015 (unpublished).
11. 'List Of Completed Video Production 1969–1979' (London), John Hopkins [JH] / Sue Hall [SH] (TVX / CATS / Fantasy Factory), British Artists' Film and Video Study Collection (retrieved 8 October 2014).
12. Ibid.
13. 'Communications Breakdown', *Time Out*, 1974, p. 11 (article appears in exhibition catalogue for *The Video Show*. The Serpentine Gallery, 1975).
14. Similar consultations today pay lip-service to the needs of those most impacted by awful housing conditions, while continuing to lead to 'decanting', pulling residents out of their neighbourhoods and disconnecting them from their communities.
15. Interview with Sue Hall by Ed Webb-Ingall, London, July, 2015 (unpublished).
16. Ibid.
17. Ibid.
18. *Community Media: Community Communication in the UK*, p. 45.
19. 'Fantasy Factory List of completed video productions 1969–1979' (accessed at Central St Martins Study Collection, London, February, 2015).
20. Heinz Nigg and Andy Porte, interview with John White, 2014. www.the-lcva.co.uk.
21. Nigg and Wade, *Community Media*, p. 47
22. The group, formed in 2013, hold meetings twice a month to work together on homelessness applications, appeals and repeals to the council, court cases, overcrowding issues, problems with temporary accommodation allowance and other housing needs.
23. Lizbeth Goodman, *Contemporary Feminist Theatres to Each Her Own* (London: Routledge, 2003), p. 266.
24. Ibid.
25. Ann Considine and Robyn Slovo, *Dead Proud: From Second Wave Young Women Playwrights* (Women's Press, 1987), p. 125.
26. Ibid., p. 1.
27. Taken from the introduction to *A Netful of Holes* (1987).

28. 'Diaspora Culture and the Dialogic Imagination: The Aesthetics of Black Independent Film in Britain'. In Kobena Mercer, *Welcome to the Jungle: New Positions in Black Cultural Studies* (London: Routledge, 1994), pp. 62, 66.
29. London Renters Union (LRU) is a London-wide, member-led campaigning union, which organises and builds solidarity between private renters across London.
30. Jackie Shaw and Clive Robertson, *Participatory Video: A Practical Guide to Using Video Creatively in Group Development Work* (London: Routledge, 1997).
31. *The Worker*, 22 Nov. 1929, p. 7.
32. Korea Senda & Heinz Lüdecke (1931), 'Agitpropisierung des proletarischen Films', *Arbeiterbühne und Film*, Vol. 18, No.5 (May): p. 10.
33. Reel News Website, 'About Us', *https://www.reelnews.co.uk/about-us* (accessed 24 June 2024).
34. What has followed is the formation of more specifically news media networks and cooperatives, including the alternative media cooperative The Media Fund (themediafund.org) that is made up of about 45 left-leaning or alternative organisations including The Canary, Novara Media and Union News. See also the Radical Film Network, founded in the UK in 2013 by a group of activists, academics and filmmakers to support the development, growth and sustainability of radical film culture. It is now the largest network for activist and experimental film in the world.

CHAPTER 4

1. Frances J. Berrigan (1975), *Theories and Practices of Video Work* (Middlesex Polytechnic: Media Research Group), pp. 11–12.
2. John Hopkins et al., *Video in Community Development*, p. 69 .
3. In the spirit of activist video projects, this chapter contains practical information and guidance that I hope continues to contribute to the making of new activist video projects.
4. Examples of these can be found in West London Media Workshop and Graft On!.
5. Bill Nichols, in Thomas Waugh, *Show Us Life: Toward a History and Aesthetics of the Committed Documentary* (Metuchen, NJ: Scarecrow, 1984), p. 138.
6. Ibid.
7. Margaret Dickinson, *Rogue Reels: Oppositional Film Making in Britain, 1945–90* (London: BFI, 1999), p. 229.
8. Nigg and Wade, *Community Media*, p. 139.

9. The film that Liberation Films produced as a document of the process was shown on BBC Two as part of the *Open Door* series, followed by a panel discussion with members of Liberation Films and the participants of the project.
10. John Hopkins et al., *Video in Community Development*, p. 113.
11. Ibid., p. 113.
12. Ibid., p. 113
13. Ibid. p. 111
14. Su Braden, *Artists and People* (London: Routledge and Kegam Paul, 1978), p. 178.
15. *Things That Mother Never Told Us!* (1979) is another example of a hybrid video project.
16. Su Braden, *Artists and People*, p. 119.
17. Ibid.
18. Graham Wade, *Street Video* (Pickering: Blackthorn Press, 1980), p. 62 .
19. Ibid., p. 60
20. Ibid., p. 67
21. Ibid., p. 71
22. Caroline Heller (1978), 'The Resistible Rise of Video Culture', *Educational Broadcasting International*, Vol. 11, No. 3 (Sep.): pp. 133–5 .
23. Ibid.
24. Ibid.
25. Interview with ED Berman by Heinz Nigg and Andy Porter, 2016. https://the-lcva.co.uk/interviews/59491ac45f88a62a1369e89c (accessed 7 Aug. 2025).
26. Ibid.
27. Ibid.

CHAPTER 5

1. Margaret Thatcher, interviewed in *World in Action* (ITV, tx. 30/1/1978).
2. Under Section 4 of the 1824 Vagrancy Act, police officers had the discretionary power to arrest anyone they suspected of loitering with intent to commit an arrestable offence. In 1978, a report by the race equality thinktank the Runnymede Trust charted the increased use of these 'Sus' laws to police Blackness. A disproportionate number of racialised arrests were being carried out, specifically the stopping and searching of black youth in urban centres, who were being arrested, charged and convicted for doing nothing more than walking down the street.
3. Ian Aitken, *The Concise Routledge Encyclopedia of the Documentary Film* (London: Routledge, 2013), p. 123 .

4. Transcript of Interview with Menelik Shabazz by Heinz Nigg and Andy Porter, 2015, https://the-lcva.co.uk/interviews/5a046328e63e3201cc7c43e9 (accessed August 2017).
5. Isaac Julien and Kobena Mercer, 'De Margin and De Center' in Houston Baker, Manthia Diawara & Ruth Lindeborg (eds), *Black British Cultural Studies: A Reader*, (London: University of Chicago Press, 1996), p. 196.
6. Chris Weedon, *Identity and Culture: Narratives of Difference and Belonging* (London: Open University Press, 2004), p. 65.
7. Inequalities in representation were also geographically biased, with the majority of funding and support located in London. In 1984 the Arts Council's 'Glory of the Garden' report recommended a ten-year strategy to redress inequitable funding between London and the regions. Both Channel 4 and the British Film Institute provided grants for video projects that encouraged the spread of activist video production into regions outside of London, and a greater diversity of experiences began to be represented on both sides of the camera. The focus of activist videos shifted and video cameras were not only directed towards race and ethnicity, but other communities of interest and identity. A number of new video groups emerged, organised around sexuality, gender and disabilities.
8. Lester D. Friedman, *Unspeakable Images: Ethnicity and the American Cinema*, University of Illinois Press, 1991. p. 149.
9. Isaac Julien & Kobena Mercer, 'De Margin and De Center', p. 201.
10. Ibid., p. 198.
11. Email interview with Andy Porter by Ed Webb-Ingall, unpublished (Dec. 2017).
12. Transcript of Interview with Isaac Julien by Tony Dowmunt, UK, 2015, www.the-lcva.co.uk (accessed August, 2017).
13. Ibid.
14. Nicholas Timmins, 'Why Colin Roach's death left legacy of unrest', *The Times*, 28 January 1983, p. 5.
15. Transcript of Interview with Isaac Julien by Tony Dowmunt
16. Transcript of Interview with Tony Dowmunt by Heinz Nigg and Andy Porter, UK, 2015, www.the-lcva.co.uk (accessed August, 2017).
17. Isaac Julien, "'There's a Conversation That's Gone Wrong, That Hasn't Been Listened to.'", 17 June 2020. www.royalacademy.org.uk/article/black-lives-matter-colin-roach-isaac-julien (accessed 3 Mar. 2024).
18. 'De Margin and De Center', p. 196.

19. Reece Auguiste, 'Handsworth Songs: Some Background Notes' in *Framework*, No. 35 (1988), p. 7.
20. Ibid., p. 5.
21. Transcript of Interview with Mark Saunders by Heinz Nigg and Andy Porter, UK, 2015, www.the-lcva.co.uk (accessed August 2017).
22. Sunil Manghani, 'The Pleasures of (Music) Video'. In Gina Arnold (ed.), *Music/Video: Histories, Aesthetics, Media*, (London: Bloomsbury, 2017), p. 25.
23. Andy Lipman, 'Scratch and Run' in *City Limits*, Oct. 1984, pp. 18–19.
24. Transcript of Interview with Isaac Julien by Tony Dowmunt.
25. Transcript of Interview with Menelik Shabazz by Heinz Nigg and Andy Porter.
26. Ibid.
27. Menelik Shabazz (2014), 'Breaking Point: The Story Behind the Film' (https://menelikshabazz.co.uk/breaking-point-story-behind-the-film (accessed May 2024).
28. Ibid.
29. Ibid.
30. Ibid.
31. Kobena Mercer, *Welcome to the Jungle: New Positions in Black Cultural Studies* (London: Routledge, 1994), p. 53 .
32. Transcript of Interview with Menelik Shabazz.
33. This footage can be seen in *Handsworth Songs* (John Akomfrah, 1986) and in Sankofa Film and Video films of the era.
34. Ibid.
35. Isaac Julien, '"There's a Conversation That's Gone Wrong, That Hasn't Been Listened to."'
36. Transcript of Interview with Menelik Shabazz.
37. Individual groups were responsible for choosing what to video, and then the raw footage was sent or brought to London, where post-production was centralised by Platform Films and largely carried out at London Video Arts, an organisation with its roots at the Dairy in Camden, where John 'Hoppy' Hopkins had first set up the video workshop TVX in the early 1970s.
38. Chris Reeves, 'Redressing the Balance: Making the *Miners' Campaign Tapes*' in booklet included with DVD release *The Miners' Campaign Tapes* (BFI, 2009), p. 8.
39. Ibid.
40. Cited in Margaret Dickinson, *Rogue Reels: Oppositional Film Making in Britain, 1945–90* (London: BFI, 1999) p. 189

CHAPTER 6

1. Interview with Paul O'Connor by Ed Webb-Ingall.
2. Ibid.
3. These websites were supported by experienced alternative media groups, including Indymedia I-contact, pirate tv, squall and schnews.
4. *ONS General Household Survey 1988–89* (London: HMSO, 1989).
5. *Framed Youth: Revenge of the Teenage Perverts* was made in 1982/83, but broadcast as part of Channel 4's *The Eleventh Hour* on 1 December 1986.
6. https://www.legislation.gov.uk/ukpga/1988/9/section/28/enacted?view=plain (accessed 4 November 2024).
7. Interview with Mark Harriott by Ed Webb-Ingall, 2019, unpublished
8. OUTRAGE!, *OutRage!*, outrage.org.uk/about (accessed 21 May 2024).
9. Thomas Harding, *The Video Activist Handbook* (London: Pluto Press, 2001), p. xiv.
10. 'undercurrents Alternative News Video Issue 1', *undercurrents Video Productions*, www.undercurrents.org/altvideos.html (accessed 3 Mar. 2024).
11. Thomas Harding, *The Video Activist Handbook,* p. xv.
12. Ibid., p. 65
13. By 1988, video coding standards produced H.120, which later became H.264, always with the aim of being able to compress moving images so that they could be transmitted within the existing bandwidth limitations while minimising loss of quality. By 1991, the Motion Pictures Expert Group developed MPEG-1 to compress VHS quality video and by 1994 MPEG-2/H.262 became the standard compression format for DVD and Standard Definition Television, and in 1999 MPEG-4/H.263 increased the capacity for Video on Demand.
14. *UK Indymedia – IMC UK About Us*, 25 June 2003, www.indymedia.org.uk/en/static/about_us.html (accessed 3 Mar. 2024).
15. Ibid.
16. 'IMC UK Mission Statement', *UK Indymedia – IMC UK Mission Statement*, 25 June 2003, www.indymedia.org.uk/en/static/mission.html (accessed 3 Mar. 2024).
17. Interview with Paul O'Connor by Ed Webb-Ingall.
18. Ibid.
19. See the 1975 Serpentine Gallery exhibition 'The Video Show', which was the first time in the UK video art and activist video projects were shown together in the context of a major institution.

20. Stuart Marshall Interviewed on *Gayblevision* (Canada: West End Community Cable, tx. 4/7/1983).
21. Ibid.
22. Ibid.

EPILOGUE

1. Raymond Williams, *Television: Technology and Cultural Form* (New York: Schocken, 1975)
2. Hannah Black, 'Social Life'. In *Text Zur Kunst*, June 2015, www.textezurkunst.de/98/social-life (accessed 3 Mar. 2024.

INDEX

Index entries in **bold** indicate illustrations.

#MeToo 161

A
A Plague on You: AIDS, the Media and the Truth (1985) 158
Abell, Tom 141, 142, 145
action tapes 70–1, 72, 74, 79
Active Image 130
AIDS 7, 141, 158–9
Albany Video 72, 74, 77, 93, 102, 105, 115, 122, 126
Alexander, Karen 74
All You Need's an Excuse (1972) 166
All-Lewisham Campaign against Racism and Fascism 105
Alternate Media Centre 30
Amazing Story of Talacre, The (1971) 166
Amber Films 18, 54, 130
Ampex 26, 32
Angry Arts Film Society 85, 86
Arts Council, the 23, 26, 54, 174
Arts Lab 20–4, **22**, **23**, 26, **27**, 100, 107
Association of Cinematograph, Television and Allied Technicians (ACTT) 107, 171
Attenborough, David 39, 42
Attille, Martina 116
Aug 13: What Happened? (1977) 102, **104**, **106**, **107**, 114, 122, **124**, 125, 126–7, 166
Auguiste, Reece 117
Avon Community Communications Association 51

B
Bakari, Imruh Caesar 111, 121
Basement Project, the 54, 170
Basic Video in Community Work (1975 publication) **32**, **39**, **71**, 82, **83**

Battle for Powis Square, The (1974) 167
BBC 27–9, 39, 40, 42, 43, 45, 48, 53, 59, 64, 86, 131, 149
Beatles, the 20, 26, 31
Ben's Arrest (1974) 61
Berman, ED 100
Betamax 149
Bhabha, Homi K. 111
Big Flame 112–13, 119
Birmingham Film and Video Workshop 18, 130
Black Audio Film Collective 109, 116, 117
Black Homelessness (1978) 167
Black Lives Matter 102, 127, 161
Black WITCH 109, 116
Black, Hannar 162
Blackfriars Photography Project 54
Blackie, the (community arts group) 54
Blackwood, Maureen 116
Boateng, Paul 121
Braden, Su 7, 48, 92
Brady, Darren 141
Breaking Point (1978) **120**, 121
Bright Eyes (1984) 159
Bristol Channel (cable television service) 18, 43, 48, 170
British Film Institute (BFI) 107, 174
Brixton uprising (1981) 122
Broadwater Farm uprising (1985) 122, 125
Broughton, Zoe 149
Bryan, Milton 121

C
Camden Housing Film for Camden Council (1972) 67
Campaign against Racism in the Media, the 40

cancel culture 162
Carnival Against Capitalism (1999) **135**, 136, **137**, 155
Ceddo Film and Video Workshop 102, 109, 111, 116, 121–3, 125
Centre for Advanced Television Studies (CATS) 11, 13, 27, 30
Challenge for Change 30, 66
Challenger, Vusi 121
Channel 40 18, 43, 44, 45, 47
Channel Four 18, 107, 108, 110, 116, 121, 122, 131, 140, 159, 170, 174
Chapter Community Video Workshop 130
Cinema Action 60, 130
Cock Crazy or Scared Stiff (1992) 158, **159**
Community Media: Community Communication in the UK (1980 report) 36
Community Programme Unit (BBC) 38–40, 42, 43, 142, 146, 170
Community Video 1980 (1980) **56**, **84**, 167
Community Video Workshop Cardiff 17
Compromised Immunity (1987) 158
Conservative Party, the 38, 43, 53, 78, 104
Cooper, Leroy 105
Covid-19 pandemic 73–4
Criminal Justice Act 1991 148, 150
Crockford, Sue 86
Crusz, Robert 116
Curtis, David 7, 22
Cybernetic Serendipity (1969 exhibtion) 134
Cybernetics 134, 135

D
Daley, Lazell 121
damp tapes 71–2, 74, 161
Dampbusters (1990) 73
Davis, D. Elmina 121
Despite TV (1982–89) 51–3, **52**, **53**
Dey, Shaun 81
Disabling Council, The (1987) **15**
Do You Love Me? (1970) 167
Don't Talk Wet – Dry Up (1983) 73
Dowmunt, Tony 7, 19, 115
Dropkin, Greg 93, 95, 96
Duggan, Mark **128**
DVD 145

E
E1 Festival (1974) 167
Easthall Residents' Association 73
Eccleston, Sukai 121
Edinburgh Workshop Trust 130

Eleventh Hour, The (1982–88) 140
End of a Tactic (1969) 86, 166
Extinction Rebellion 161

F
Familiar Feelings (1982) **17**
Federation of Workers Film Societies, the 16, 80
Fight the Cuts (1979) 167
film collectives 16
Films at Work 130
Floyd, George 127
Fly a Flag for Poplar (1974) 167
Forensic Architecture 128
Forming a Residents Association (1974) 68–70, 69, 166
Framed Youth: Revenge of the Teenage Perverts (1983) **14**, **56**, **140**, 141, 146, 166
Frost Programme, The (1966–73) **28**, 29, 166
Frostbite (1970) 166

G
G8 summit 136
Gay Sweatshop 141
Gilroy, Paul 111
Givanni, June 109
Gorney, Carry 7, 45–6, **49**
Graft On! 61, 65–6, 66, 68, 70, 77, 93, 172
Greater London Council (GLC) 52, 72, 110
Greenwich Cablevision 18, 43, **46**
Grierson, John 117
Gupta, Sunil 158
Gutzmore, Cecil 125

H
Half Moon (community arts group) 54
Hall, Stuart 42, 111, 121
Hall, Sue 7, 61, 64, 65, 67, 68, 70
Handsworth Songs (1986) **109**, **117**, 166, 175
Handsworth uprising (1981) 18, 23, 106, 117, 122
happenings 20
Hard Stop, The (2016) 127, 128, 166
Harding, Thomas 149, 150, 153
Harriott, Mark 7, 141–2, 143, 144, 145
Hartzell, Jamie 149–50
Hayling, Alan 113
Haynes, Jim 20, 22, 24
Hinton, Jeffrey 141
Homes for the People (1945) 60
Hopkins, John 'Hoppy' 7, 24–9, **25**, 30, 61, 63, 65, 66–7, 68, 69, 171, 175
Hostile Housing (2019) 76, 77

Housing Action Southwark and Lambeth (HASL) 73, 172
Housing Problems (1935) **60**
How to Use a Portapack (1978) 166

I
Ikoli, Tunde 54
Imarogbe, Dada 121
IMC United Kollektives 156
Immigration and Deportation (1980) 95
Independent Broadcasting Authority (IBA) 121, 125
Independent Filmmakers' Association 107
Indymedia 81, 155–6, 175
Instagram 102, 134, 161, 162
Institute for Research and Technology (IRAT) 26, 27, 65
Institute of Contemporary Arts (ICA) 134
Institute of Mass Communications Research 27
Inter-Action 45, **56**, 82, **97**, 100–1, **101**, 119
Inter-Action Media Van (1974) 100–1, 166
International Monetary Fund 155
International Times 24
Into the Darkness (1977) 166
Isaac, Julien 7, 102–3, 112–16, 117, 118, 119, 126, 127, 158
ITV 121, 131

J
Jarrett, Cynthia 122, 125
Jarrett, Floyd 123
Jeffrey, David 22
Jenkins, Julie 141
Jones, Bob 95
Just Stop Oil 161

K
Kaposi's Sarcoma: A Plague and its Symptoms (1983) 158
Kaprow, Allan 20
Kino 81
Know Your Rights (activist group) 102
Kuumba Productions 111

L
Labour Party, the 61, 67, 155
Lennon, John 20, 26
Liberation Films 81, 85–92, **85**, **88**, 98, 173
Little Picture Show, The (1993–95) 151
Liverpool Black Media Group 109, 116
Livin' Free (1972) 67

Living Rent 65
Lockdown Diaries (2020) **75**
London Film-makers' Co-operative 22, 26, 107, 120
London Renters Union (LRU) 77, 172
London Video Arts 158, 175

M
M11 campaign 146, 149–51
MacDowell, Noreen 113
Manchester Film and Video Workshop 17, 93, **94**, 95, **96**
March to Aldermaston (1959) 166
Marshall, Stuart 158, 159
Marsh-Edwards, Nadine 116
Masokonane, Glenn Ujebe 121
Mayday 2000 actions 156
Media Fund, the 172
Media Workshop Belfast 17
Mercer, Kobena 111, 116, 122
Metropolitan Police 105, 143
Miners' Campaign Tapes, The (1984–85) 130–1, **130**, 142, 166
Miners' Strike (1984–85) 130–1, 146
Moore, Jack Henry 20, 22, 24
Mosley, Oswald 104
Mosside uprising 106
Murcheson Tenants (c.1977) 167

N
National Coal Board 130
National Film Board of Canada 30
National Front 102, 104–5
National Union of Mineworkers (NUM) 130
Netful of Holes, A (1984) 74, 77, 172
News at West 10 (1976–77) 34–7, **35**, **37**, **38**, 167
Newsreel 85–6
Newsreel Collective 113
Ngakane, Lionel 111
North Kenton Residents Group 73
Not a Penny on The Rents (1968) 60
Notting Hill demo (1969) 25
Nottingham Video Project 130

O
O'Connor, Paul 7, 136, 146–9, **150**, 155, 157, 169
O'Malley, Jan 61
Ono, Yoko 20
Open Door (1973–83) 40–2, **41**, 45, 167, 169, 173
Open Eye Film and Video Workshop 130
Open Space (1983–95) 158, 169
Operation Swamp 105

Other Cinema, The 120
Out on Tuesday / Out (1989–94) 140
OUTRAGE! 142–4, 156, 158
OUTRAGE! Tapes (1993–94) **143**, 166
Oval Video 115
Ové, Horace 111
Over Our Dead Bodies (1991) 159

P
Pan African Cinema Archive 109
Parmar, Pratibha 159
People's Account, The (1985) 102, **108**, **112**, 122–5, **122**, **123**, **124**, 126, 127–8, 166
Pepys Estate – Organising (1974) **73**, 167
Pepys Estate Repairs Campaign (1974) 167
Pinhorn, Maggie 54
Pink Floyd 24
Platform Films 130, 131, 175
Please Adjust Your Eyes 166
Porter, Andy 7, 34, 72, 111, 172
POUT (1992–94) 138–42, **139**, 144–6, **145**, **147**, **148**, 156, 158, 166
Pressure (1975) **110**
process tapes 70
Project Octopus 87–92

Q
Quadruplex 32

R
Radical Film Network 172
Raindance Corporation 30
Real Time 77
Reel News (2006-) 81
Reeves, Chris 131
Reframing AIDS (1987) 159
Reid, June 121
Release UK 102
Retake 109, 116
Richman, Geoff 86, 87
Richman, Marie 86
Right to Buy 78
Roach, Colin 113–14, 116, 123
Roberts, Amanda 141
Robertson, Clive 77
Rolling Stones, the 20, 70
Rubin, Jerry 29

S
Sankofa Film and Video Collective 109, 116, 175
Saunders, Mark 51, 52, 118
Scarman Report (1981) 110

scratch video 117–18, 141
Second Wave 74, 75, 77
Section 28 141, 142
Sembène, Ousemane 122
Shabazz, Menelik 109, 111, 119–21, 122, 125, 128, 129
Shaw, Jackie 77
Sheffield Cablevision 18, **43**, 51
Sheffield Video Workshop 17
Small World Media 150, 151
Snapchat 134
Song of Long Ago (1975) 166
Sony 11–13, 25, 26, 32–3
Sony Portapak 24, 29, 32–3, 93, 95, 96, 101, 109, 119, 162
Sony TCV-2010 11, **12**
Southwark Council Make Empty Flats on Aylesbury Estate Uninhabitable (2015) 58, 59
Speak Out about Safer Sex (1991) 159
Squat Now While Stocks Last (1974) 61–3, **62**, 166, 171
Squatters (1970) 60
Starting to Happen (1974) **13**, **56**, 87–8, **89**, **90**, **92**, 98, 167
Steed, Maggie 42
Step Forward Youth (1977) 120, 166
Stevens, Andrew 141
Stevens, Carol 74
Stopwatch 102
Street Video (1980 publication) 96
Sus laws 120, 173
Sweet 16 (1977) 166
Swindon Cable **47**
Swindon Viewpoint 18, 43, 51
Swingbridge Media 73

T
Tawadros, Gilane 111
Thatcher, Margaret 78, 104, 116, 118, 130
Theories and Practices of Video Work (1975 report) 82
Things That Mother Never Told Us! (1979) 46–8, **50**, 51, 166, 173
This is Not an AIDS Advertisement (1987) 158
TikTok 134
Time Out (magazine) 64, 151
Timmins, Philip 158
Toxteth uprising 1981 105
Trade Films 130
Tribute to Black Women (They Don't Get a Chance) (1986) **115**
trigger films 89–90, 92, 95

True Romance (1982) 113, 166
Tunde's Film (1973) 54, **55**
TVX 27–30, 67, 120, 175
Tweneboa, Kwajo 161
Twitter (now X) 74

U
Ukpabi, Chuma 121
U-matic 131
undercurrents (1994–99) 136–9, **138**, 146, 150–7, **151**, **152**, **154**, **157**, 161

V
VHS 51, 105, 118, 131, 138, 141, 142, 145, 155, 167
Video Active (1985 report) 51, 52
Video Activist Handbook, The (1991 publication) 153
Video Diaries (1990–99) 146, 148–9, **149**
Video in Community Development (1972 publication) 11, 13, 30, 89, 91
Video Nation (1993–2001) 169
Video Space (1970) **21**, 27–8, 167
Vietnam Solidarity Campaign (VSC) 86
Vietnam War 14, 81
VTR St-Jacques (1969) 166

W
Watchful Eye 58, 63, 65

Wellingborough Cablevision 18, 43, 51
West London Media Workshop (WLMW) 34–5, 36, 52, 93, 111–2, 172
White Defence League 104
White, John 7, 29, 72, 104
Whitehouse, Mary 29
Who Killed Colin Roach? (1983) 102, 103, 113–6, **113**, **114**, **124**, 125, 126, 127, 166
Wickert, Tony 7, 86
Williams, Raymond 161
Windrush generation 104
WITCH (Women's IndependenT Cinema House) 109
Woman's Place, A (1971) 86, **87**, 167
women's movement 45–6, 47, 86
Workers Newsreel 81
Workshop Declaration 18, 107–8, 116, 121, 170
World Bank 155

Y
Young, Lola 125
Youth International Party ('Yippies') 29
YouTube 81, 134
Y-Stop 102

Z
Zappa, Frank 28

ILLUSTRATION CREDITS

While considerable effort has been made to correctly identify copyright holders, this has not been possible in all cases. Where no rights holder is listed, the image is understood to be out of copyright. Any omissions or corrections brought to our attention will be remedied in any future editions. The majority of images are sourced from digitised films and videos from the London Community Video Archive (LCVA) and the BFI National Archive and from the LCVA's digitised paper collections.

Starting to Happen – **pp.13**, **57**, **89**, **90**, **92**, playback/screenings – **pp.85**, **89**, *Liberation Films Distribution Catalogue* – **p.133** © Liberation Films; *Pepys Estate Organising* – **p.73**; *Aug 13: What Happened* – **pp.104**, **106**, **107**, **124** © Albany Video; News at W.10 flyer – **p.35**, News at West 10 playback – **p.37**, News at West 10 van screening – **p.38** © West London Media Workshop; *Basic Video in Community Work* – **pp.32–3**, **39**, **57**, **71**, **83**, Inter-Action kids/adults workshops – **p.57**, Inter-Action media van – **p.101** © Inter-Action; *Video Space* – **p.21** © John Hopkins; *Arts Lab workers* – **p.22** © David Kilburn/Tate Archive; John 'Hoppy' Hopkins – **p.25** © The Hoppy Hopkins Archive/Bishopsgate Institute; *Squat Now While Stocks Last* – **p.62** © Sue Hall/Estate of John 'Hoppy' Hopkins; Carry Gorney – **p.49**, *Things That Mother Never Told Us* – **p.50** © Carry Gorney/Channel 40; *Despite TV* – **pp.52**, **53** © Mark Saunders – Despite TV; *Framed Youth: Revenge of the Teenage Perverts* – **pp.14**, **57**, **140** © Lesbian and Gay Youth Video Project; *Community Video 1980* – **p.57**, **84** © Joel Venet; *Southwark Council make empty flats on Aylesbury Estate uninhabitable* – **pp.61**, **63**, *Fight for the Aylesbury* – **p.61** © Watchful Eye; Video as an Analytic Tool – **p.66**, *Forming a Residents Association* – **p.71** © Graft On!; *Who Killed Colin Roach?* – **pp.103**, **113**, **114**, **124** © Isaac Julien; *The People's Account* – **pp.108**, **112**, **122**, **123**, **124** © Ceddo Film and Video Workshop; *Step Forward Youth* – **p.119**, *Breaking Point* – **p.120** © Menelik Shabazz; *Handsworth Songs* – **pp.109**, **117** © Smoking Dogs Films; *undercurrents Alternative News Video* – **pp.138**, **149**, **152**, **154**, **155**, **157** © undercurrents; Small World Media edit suite – **p.136** © Paul O'Connor/undercurrents; *Reclaim the Streets* – **p.150** © Paul O'Connor; *POUT* – **pp.139**, **143**, **145**, **147** © Mark Harriott/POUT Collective; *OUTRAGE! Tapes* – **p.144** © Mark Harriott; Sony TCV-2010 Videocorder – **p.12** © Sony Group Corporation; *The Disabling Council* – **p.15**; *Familiar Feelings* – **p.17** © Common Stock Youth Theatre; *The New Arts Lab Robert Street* – **p.27** © Pamela Zoline; *The Frost Programme* – **p.28** © ITV; *Open Door* – **p.41**, *Video Diaries* – **p.149** © BBC; Sheffield Cablevision camerawoman – **p.43** © Sheffield Cablevision; Greenwich Cablevision Shopfront – **p.46** © Greenwich Cablevision; Swindon Cable mixing desk – **p.47** © Swindon Cable; *Tunde's Film* – **p.55** © Basement Project Film Group; *Lockdown Diaries* – **p.75** © Housing Action Southwark & Lambeth; *Hostile Housing* – **p.76** © London Renters Union; *Orgreave Truth & Justice Campaign* – **p.80** © Reel News; Manchester Film and Video Workshop – **pp.94**, **96** © Manchester Film and Video Workshop/Graham Wade; *Pressure* – **p.110** © BFI; *A Tribute to Black Women (They don't get a chance)* – **p.115** © Ann Carney and Barbara Phillips/Black Women's Media Project & WITCH; *Rendering of the moment Duggan steps out of the minicab* – **p.128** © Forensic Architecture; *The Miners' Campaign Tapes* – **p.130** © The Miners' Campaign Tapes; *East End on Screen* – **p.133** © Tower Hamlets Arts Project Books; *Directory of Video Tapes* – **p.133** © London Community Video Workers; *Catalogue of Films and Videos Directed by Women* – **p.133** © Circles/COW/Cinenova; *Carnival Against Capitalism* – **pp.135**, **137** © Indymedia; *Cock Crazy or Scared Stiff* – **p.159** © Sunil Gupta.